Ivy Bake Shoppe

C O O K B O O K

MARTHA WOLF

Ivy Bake Shoppe

COOKBOOK

Gibbs Smith, Publisher

to enrich and inspire humankind

Salt Lake City | Charleston | Santa Fe | Santa Barbara

First Edition
11 10 09 08 07   5 4 3 2

Published by
Gibbs Smith, Publisher
P.O. Box 667
Layton, Utah 84041

Orders: 1.800.835.4993
www.gibbs-smith.com

Designed by Blackeye Design
Printed and bound in Korea

Library of Congress Cataloging-in-Publication Data
Wolf, Martha.
  Ivy Bake Shoppe cookbook / Martha Wolf. — 1st ed.
    p. cm.
  ISBN-13: 978-1-4236-0191-3
  ISBN-10: 1-4236-0191-2
  1. Baking. 2. Cookery. 3. Ivy Bake Shoppe & Cafe. I. Title.

TX765.W65 2007
641.8'15—dc22

                    2006031222

To the honor of our mothers, Elinor Welch and Hannah Hatfield, we dedicate this book. Their strong, faith-based lives have sustained us and given us the courage to face the many challenges with which we have been confronted.

Their recipes of life:

- Say your prayers daily
- Love your family
- Nurture those around you
- Always make people feel special
- If it is worth doing, it is worth doing right
- Find the positive no matter the circumstance
- Observe and treasure life daily

We live the life we are given. Our mothers showed us by example to take the opportunities we are given and be open to all the possibilities that life has to offer us. We truly treasure the blessings each customer brings to the Ivy Bake Shoppe and Cafe.

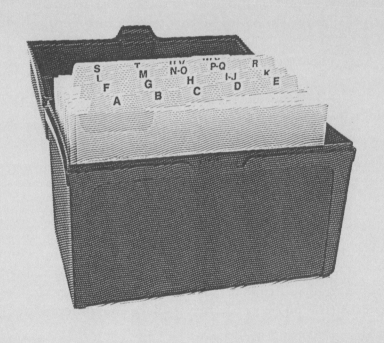

contents

 acknowledgments

These Ivy recipes stand the test of time. People often ask where we get all of our recipes. We are blessed to have great cooks in our families that readily share all of their secrets. After reading trade magazines, we often make up recipes based on a chef's description, a menu item, or a picture. We have also been fortunate to have friends, and even customers, share great recipes with us. We acknowledge that all of these recipes are not ours, and we so appreciate people's generosity in sharing them. They are our favorites.

We also want to take this opportunity to thank our three former partners and long-time friends—Kathy Carton, Dodie Jerome, and Holly Ritter—who shared in the hard work and entrepreneurial spirit of, and dedication to, our business. Without their timely efforts, the Ivy would never have become a reality. We will always be grateful for their continued support over the last ten years.

——— the ivy ———

It feeds the body, nourishes the mind, and satisfies the soul.

As you read this cookbook, I hope you will keep in mind that I am only one of a partnership; and although I am writing the story, Sue Saunders has lived through it all right by my side. She is organized, detail-oriented, and deliberate. I am a procrastinator, disorganized, and will promise the world but only deliver on that promise after Sue writes a note to remind me.

Sue moved to Fort Madison in 1967 with her husband, who had just finished law school. I moved to Fort Madison in 1972 for a job as a social worker in protective services. We both settled into this small town and have called it home ever since.

Fort Madison, Iowa, is a Mississippi River town, rich in history, having begun as a territorial fort in 1808. In the 1920s, Santa Fe Railroad built the world's largest swing span bridge in Fort Madison. Fort Madison is also home to the Sheaffer

Pen Company, inventor of the lever-filled fountain pen. All of these accomplishments contributed to the construction of elegant Victorian-inspired homes. Many of these prominent homes remain today, giving Fort Madison a noticeable 1890s atmosphere.

Once we had decided to start the Ivy, trying to name it was one of the more difficult jobs. In Sue's kitchen with several friends, we sat around the table tossing about names; some were cutesy or catchy, others real groaners, but several good possibilities. However, none of them were quite "it." Sue was in the process of opening a bed-and-breakfast in her home, to be called The Ivy Manor. The name reflected her three-story Victorian home covered in ivy. Since we started in the lower level of Sue's home, a friend suggested keeping the ivy theme. Hence, the Ivy was born.

The Ivy Bake Shoppe and Cafe is now located in historic downtown, a five-block area that is vibrant and alive. Though Fort Madison is a small town, we have numerous specialty shops and retail stores that offer great service, customer satisfaction, and a sincere desire to make a difference.

People have now been visiting the Ivy since 1995. Most people discovered us by word of mouth. Customers walked in the door, never having been here before, but knowing they were going to order the Warm Onion Pie, Tortilla Soup, Caramel Rice Krispie Treat, or Caramel Apple Tart. They returned whenever they could because, as a customer once said, "It's like coming home." Every day the Ivy is open is a testament to the power and strength of nurtured relationships and the blessings and gifts that accompany them.

 treats

Raised on the Gulf Coast of Mississippi, I was the youngest of seven children. Early recollections of my food history are of my mother's cooking. After she got my siblings off to school, we would go "crabbing" on the Gulf of Mexico piers, return home, and throw the live crabs into boiling water; then I would watch her make a rich, wonderful gumbo for dinner that night. Or perhaps we would head north of Gulfport to a friend's farm and pick dewberries in the pasture, and mother would fix fresh dewberry cobbler for dessert.

Sue's mother was also a great cook who always made mealtime special for her family. Our mothers were gracious hostesses, and Sue and I, as co-owners, have carried on that tradition at the Ivy. We have worked very hard to provide people with an incredible meal in a warm, nurturing atmosphere. We are an anchor in this community and proud to have assisted in the revitalization of downtown Fort Madison.

We are reminded every day of the memories we are creating for our customers, our staff, and ourselves. The following recipes are favorite food memories of Sue and myself from our growing-up in Mapleton, Iowa, and Gulfport, Mississippi, respectively.

DEWBERRY COBBLER

2 cups berries
  (any kind)
¾ cup sugar
1 tbsp. flour
4 tbsp. water
2 tbsp. butter, cut in pieces
1 cup flour
2 tbsp. shortening
¼ cup sugar
¼ tsp. salt
1 tbsp. baking powder
½ cup milk

Grease a 1-quart baking dish. Mix the berries, ¾ cup sugar, 1 tablespoon flour, and water together gently and then pour into a baking dish; dot with butter pieces. Cut all remaining ingredients together except the milk. When mixed, add the milk and combine until doughy. Shape dough to fit in baking dish and place over berries to cover. Bake at 350 degrees for 35 to 45 minutes. Makes 4 to 6 servings.

POUND CAKE

2 sticks butter
2 ¾ cups sugar
12 egg yolks, room
  temperature*
3 cups flour
¼ tsp. salt
¼ tsp. baking soda
1 cup buttermilk
2 tsp. pure vanilla extract

Cream butter and sugar together until the consistency of whipped cream. Add egg yolks one at a time, mixing well. Sift together flour, salt, and baking soda. Add buttermilk and flour mixture to batter alternately, stirring after each addition; stir in vanilla. Divide batter between two greased and floured loaf pans. Bake at 350 degrees for 70 minutes, or until a toothpick inserted in the center comes out clean. Freezes great! Makes 8 slices per loaf.

*Use the leftover egg whites in the Angel Food Cake on page 17.

ANGEL FOOD CAKE

Add salt and cream of tartar to egg whites in a mixing bowl with a wire whisk attachment; beat until soft peaks hold. Gradually beat in sugar, 1 tablespoon at a time, until stiff peaks form; add vanilla. Sift together flour and powdered sugar three times. Gently fold flour mixture into mixing bowl with egg whites. Mix thoroughly but carefully.

Place batter in an ungreased tube pan. Bake at 350 degrees for 40 minutes. Remove from oven and then hang upside down over the neck of a bottle until cool. Makes 12 servings.

*Use the leftover egg yolks in the Pound Cake on page 16.

½ tsp. salt
1 tsp. cream of tartar
12 egg whites, room temperature*
1 cup sugar
1 tsp. vanilla
1 cup flour
1 cup powdered sugar

BUTTERSCOTCH PIE

FILLING

1 cup firmly packed brown
   sugar
½ cup flour
¼ tsp. salt
1 (12-oz.) can evaporated
   milk
4 egg yolks, room
   temperature
½ stick butter, cut
   into pieces
1 tsp. vanilla
1 baked 9-inch pie shell

MERINGUE

¼ tsp. salt
¼ tsp. cream of tartar
4 egg whites, room
   temperature
½ cup sugar

Prepare filling by combining brown sugar, flour, and salt in a bowl. Add enough water to evaporated milk to equal 2 cups. Lightly beat egg yolks and then whisk in ½ cup of the diluted milk. Whisk the yolk mixture into the dry ingredients until thoroughly blended and then add the remaining diluted milk.

Transfer mixture to the top of a double boiler. Cook over simmering water, whisking constantly for 10 to 15 minutes or until very thick. Remove from heat and stir in butter and vanilla. Cover surface with a round of wax paper. Let cool for 15 minutes. Pour into pie shell and cover again. Let cool to room temperature and then refrigerate until well chilled, about 3 hours.

For the meringue, combine salt and cream of tartar together. Whip egg whites with salt and cream of tartar mixture until soft peaks form. Gradually add sugar, 1 tablespoon at a time, until stiff peaks form. Frost pie with meringue and then bake at 425 degrees for 12 to 15 minutes, or until meringue turns golden; cool on rack. Refrigerate at least 3 hours before serving. Makes 8 servings.

ANGEL PIE

Preheat oven to 275 degrees. Beat egg whites until frothy. Add cream of tartar and salt and beat until it holds shape. Slowly add sugar, 1 tablespoon at a time, and beat until very stiff. Spread in a buttered 10-inch pie pan, as you would a crust. Bake for 10 minutes and then turn oven off, leaving pie shell in oven for 5 hours or overnight.

To make the filling, beat egg yolks until smooth. Add sugar, lemon juice, zest, and boiling water. Cook in a double boiler until thick; cool.

Whip the cream and then place half in the bottom of baked pie shell. Pour cooled cooked mixture over this. Spread rest of whipped cream evenly over top of pie. Makes 8 servings.

4 egg whites
¼ tsp. cream of tartar
Pinch of salt
1 cup sugar

FILLING
6 egg yolks
¾ cup sugar
5 tbsp. lemon juice
1 ½ tsp. lemon zest
½ cup boiling water
1 cup heavy cream

MY MOMMA'S PRALINES VERBATIM

3 cups sugar
1 cup half-and-half
Pinch of salt
½ stick butter
2 tsp. vanilla
3 cups toasted pecans

Caramelize about ½ cup sugar by putting it in a small heavy skillet over low heat and stirring constantly until melted and amber in color. In the meantime, put remaining sugar and half-and-half in a heavy saucepan and bring to a boil, stirring constantly. Turn heat to low and add the caramelized sugar. It will froth up, but stir vigorously for a few minutes until it is all mixed together. Cook over low heat (stirring only occasionally) until candy thermometer reaches soft ball stage or 232 degrees. Take off burner and add butter and vanilla and then don't stir until it reaches 110 degrees. Then beat by hand (too thick to use beater) for about 10 minutes. Before it gets too thick, add toasted pecans. Drop onto wax paper. Instead of dropping, you can just spread on waxed paper and make a long roll, wrap, and then place in refrigerator. When completely cooled, slice. Makes 12 pralines.

CARAMELS

Combine all ingredients except vanilla and
nuts in a heavy 3- to 4-quart saucepan.
Cook over low heat, stirring occasionally,
until sugar is dissolved and butter is melted,
about 20 minutes. Continue cooking, without stirring, until mixture forms a firm ball
or 246 degrees on a candy thermometer,
about 2 hours. Heat should be low enough
to just keep a steady, low boil. Remove from
heat, stir in vanilla and nuts and then pour
onto a buttered baking sheet. Cool, cut, and
wrap in waxed paper. Makes 24 pieces.

2 cups sugar
1 cup firmly packed light
  brown sugar
1 cup butter, softened
2 cups half-and-half
1 cup light Karo syrup
½ tsp. salt
1 ¼ tsp. vanilla
1 cup chopped
  pecans, toasted

PEPPERNUTS

Sift spices, except for anise, with flour and
salt. Stir in anise.

In mixing bowl, mix sugar, corn syrup,
butter, shortening, and egg. Slowly add
some flour and then soda mixture, and then
rest of flour. Batter will be very stiff, and
final mixing will need to be by hand.

Take small amounts of batter and roll into
long strings about the size of your finger.
Arrange on a tray covered with waxed paper
and refrigerate until ready to bake.

Preheat oven to 375 degrees. Cut dough
into small pieces, about ¼ inch, and bake on
a greased pan for about 12 minutes. Makes
about 200 pieces.

1 tsp. cinnamon
1 tsp. cloves
1 tsp. allspice
½ tsp. salt
5 ½ cups flour
1 ½ tsp. anise seed (put in
  a cloth bag and pound to
  powder with a hammer)
1 cup sugar
1 cup dark corn syrup
½ cup butter
½ cup shortening
1 beaten egg
1 tsp. soda, dissolved in
  1 tbsp. coffee

FUDGE

4 cups sugar
¾ cup corn syrup
1 cup cream
3 squares unsweetened
   chocolate bar
1 stick butter, divided
1 tsp. vanilla
½ cup chopped black
   walnuts (pecans or
   English walnuts also
   work well)

Cook sugar, corn syrup, cream, and unsweetened chocolate with 4 tablespoons butter in a saucepan until it reaches 234 degrees on a candy thermometer; remove from heat. Add remaining butter and vanilla. Let cool to 110 degrees. Beat until it loses the glossy look, about 15 minutes. Add nuts and then pour into a buttered 8 x 8-inch pan. Makes 24 pieces.

NOTES

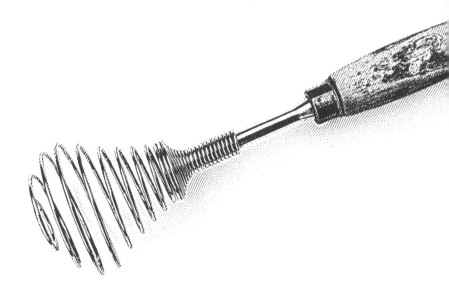

—— bars, brownies & cookies ——

Sue and I started the Ivy in 1992 with three other women. We each invested 100 dollars to cover the initial advertising costs and other small start-up fees. In the beginning, we were open every Friday morning in the lower level of Sue's home, which she had turned into a bed-and-breakfast after her divorce. Customers entered through sliding glass doors, walked through the family room and the game room, and finally to a room with a Ping-Pong table covered with our baked goods.

We were not only a very democratic group but also a very competitive one. We all made our own specialties (no duplicates allowed). When purchases were totaled, we kept track of whose food had been purchased. At the end of the month, paydays were based on everything sold less 5 percent that went into the Bake Shoppe account. We met every Monday night to discuss the previous Friday and to iron out any problems. Determination, focus, motivation, and brutal honesty made our weekly sales successful.

Timing was another notable factor in our success. Sue and I were both going through divorces and searching for new directions. Though neither of us was looking for a full-time job, we both needed to be busy and productive. Our tireless efforts to make the Ivy a success benefited our mental health as much as our bank accounts, though our bank deposits were never substantial. Realistically, we were a glorified bake sale.

To make our product available more than one day a week, we contacted Ron Boeding, owner of a small neighborhood grocery store. For a small commission, Ron placed our baked goods right by the check-out counter. With great visibility, we were stocking his shelves with our product five days a week.

In the beginning, I discovered our customers were mainly Sue's friends who felt sorry for us. After six months, I realized that even best friends have only so much freezer space. Then I noticed a remarkable trend—many of the people walking into the lower level of Sue's home to buy food were STRANGERS!

Our business was truly growing. We found a niche and it was unbelievable! People wanted home-baked food using real butter, cream, and sugar. Some had disposable income, didn't have extra time, or just wanted a quality product. Whatever the reason, they didn't mind paying extra to purchase a quality product.

Over the next eighteen months, the other three partners tired of the bake sale routine and dropped out. At this time, we supplied product three days a week to a neighborhood grocery store, a convenience store, and two retail shops. Sue focused on building her bed-and-breakfast business; and with three children at home, baking times were unpredictable for me. Our kitchens were a mess, but our emotional health was good. Sue and I were feeling successful and we were making some money.

The following recipes include some of the original sweets we sold from the Ping-Pong table, as well as some brownies and bars that we have discovered or developed later.

CHOCOLATE CARAMEL BROWNIE

Mix cake mix, butter, evaporated milk, and pecans together. Spread two-thirds of the dough mixture in a greased 9 x 13-inch pan. Bake at 350 degrees for 7 minutes.

For the caramel layer, melt caramels with evaporated milk in microwave for 3 minutes. Stir and then microwave 1 minute more; stir until smooth. Pour mixture over baked batter and then sprinkle with chocolate chips. Dot with remaining dough. Bake at 350 degrees for 10 to 12 minutes; set on a rack to cool. Cover and cool 6 hours before serving. Makes 12 to 15 servings.

1 box German chocolate cake mix
1 1/2 sticks butter, softened
1/3 cup evaporated milk
1 cup chopped pecans

CARAMEL LAYER
1 (14-oz.) bag caramels, unwrapped
1/4 cup evaporated milk
1 cup semisweet chocolate chips

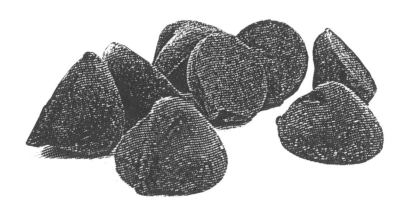

CHOCOLATE MINT BROWNIE

1 stick butter, softened
1 cup sugar
4 eggs
1 1/4 cups chocolate syrup
1 cup flour
1/2 tsp. baking powder

MINT CREAM LAYER

2 cups powdered sugar
1 stick butter, softened
2 tbsp. water
1/2 tsp. mint flavoring
2 drops green food coloring

CHOCOLATE TOPPING

1 cup semisweet
  chocolate chips
6 tbsp. butter

Beat the butter and sugar together until creamy. Add eggs and continue beating until combined. Add syrup, flour, and baking powder. Beat for 2 minutes on medium speed. Pour batter into a greased 9 x 13-inch pan. Bake at 350 degrees for 20 to 25 minutes; cool.

To make the mint cream layer, beat all the ingredients together in a bowl until light and fluffy; frost brownies and then refrigerate.

For the chocolate topping, heat ingredients in a microwave for 30 to 45 seconds; stir until smooth. Spread on top of mint layer, leaving a border of green frosting around the edges of the pan; refrigerate again. Let frosted brownies come to room temperature before cutting to serve. Makes 12 to 15 servings.

BETTER THAN A SNICKERS BAR

Melt all first layer ingredients together in microwave for 1 1/2 minutes and stir until smooth. Spread in a greased 9 x 13-inch pan; chill while making the second layer.

For the second layer, combine and cook first three ingredients for 10 minutes in a saucepan over medium heat and stir until smooth. Add marshmallow creme and peanut butter and then pour over first layer. Sprinkle peanuts over top.

For the third layer, melt ingredients together in microwave for 2 to 3 minutes and stir together until smooth. Pour over second layer and peanuts.

For the fourth layer, melt ingredients together in microwave for 1 to 1 1/2 minutes and stir together until smooth. Pour over third layer. Chill in refrigerator for several hours. Let come to room temperature before serving. Makes 12 to 16 servings.

FIRST LAYER

1 1/2 cups mini
   chocolate chips
1/4 cup butterscotch chips
1/4 cup peanut butter

SECOND LAYER

1 cup sugar
1/2 stick butter
1/4 cup evaporated milk
7 oz. marshmallow creme
1/4 cup peanut butter
1 1/2 cups cocktail peanuts

THIRD LAYER

1 (14-oz.) bag caramels,
   unwrapped
2 tbsp. evaporated milk

FOURTH LAYER

1 cup mini chocolate chips
1/4 cup peanut butter
1/4 cup butterscotch chips

MILLENNIUM TOFFEE BAR

2 1/2 cups flour
3/4 cup butter
2/3 cup packed light
  brown sugar
1 egg, slightly beaten
2 cups semisweet
  chocolate chips,
  divided
1 cup chopped pecans
1 (14-oz.) can sweetened
  condensed milk
1 3/4 cups toffee bits, divided

Grease a 9 x 13-inch glass dish. Preheat oven to 350 degrees. In a mixing bowl, mix together flour, butter, and brown sugar; add egg and mix well. Add 1 1/2 cups chocolate chips and nuts. Reserve 1 1/2 cups of the mixture. Press remaining mixture into the bottom of the pan. Bake for 8 minutes.

Remove from oven and pour sweetened condensed milk over mixture. Top with 1 1/2 cups toffee bits, the reserved crumb mixture, and 1/2 cup chocolate chips. Return to oven for 12 minutes. Remove from oven and sprinkle with remaining toffee bits. Cool before cutting, or just eat it with a spoon! Makes 12 to 16 servings.

ROCKY ROAD BROWNIE

Melt butter and unsweetened chocolate in the microwave for 45 to 60 seconds. Put in a mixing bowl and add remaining cake ingredients; beat until combined. Spread mixture into a greased 9 x 13-inch glass dish. To make the filling, beat the first six ingredients together until creamed and fluffy. Carefully spread over brownie layer in pan. Sprinkle chocolate chips on top. Bake at 350 degrees for 30 minutes. Do not overbake. Remove from oven and top with marshmallows and then return to oven for 1 to 2 minutes, or until marshmallows are puffy and beginning to turn golden.

To make the frosting, melt the first four ingredients together in the microwave for 1 1/2 minutes; stir until smooth. Place in a mixing bowl, and then slowly add the sugar; beat until smooth. Add more milk (a tablespoon at a time) for spreading consistency.

Frost brownies when you remove them from the oven. Let cool 1 to 2 hours before serving. Makes 12 to 15 servings.

1 stick butter

1 square unsweetened chocolate (1 oz.)

1 cup flour

1 cup sugar

2 eggs

1 tsp. baking powder

1 tsp. vanilla extract

1/2 cup chopped pecans

FILLING

6 oz. cream cheese, room temperature

1/2 stick butter, softened

1 egg

1/2 cup sugar

2 tbsp. flour

1/2 tsp. vanilla extract

1 cup semisweet chocolate chips

2 cups miniature marshmallows

FROSTING

1/2 stick butter

2 oz. cream cheese

1/4 cup milk

1 square unsweetened chocolate, melted (1 oz.)

4 1/3 cups powdered sugar (about 1 lb.)

FUDGE OATMEAL BAR

2 sticks butter

2 cups brown sugar

2 eggs

2 tsp. vanilla extract

2 cups flour

1 tsp. baking soda

1 tsp. salt

3 cups uncooked oatmeal

FILLING

2 cups milk
chocolate chips

1 can sweetened
condensed milk

1 tbsp. butter

1/2 tsp. salt

2 tsp. vanilla extract

With an electric mixer, cream butter and sugar together; add eggs and mix thoroughly. Stir in remaining ingredients. Spread two-thirds of batter in a greased 10 x 15-inch jellyroll pan. Set reserved batter aside.

For the filling, melt the ingredients together in a microwave for 1 minute. Stir and microwave 30 seconds longer; mixture should be smooth. Spread filling over batter in pan. Sprinkle reserved oatmeal batter in small clumps over the surface. Bake at 350 degrees for 25 to 30 minutes. Makes 16 to 20 servings.

CARAMEL RICE KRISPIES BAR

Place caramels, sweetened condensed milk, and butter in a bowl and microwave for 3 minutes. Stir until smooth, returning to microwave if not yet melted; set aside to cool.

In another bowl, melt 6 tablespoons of butter with 4 cups marshmallows for 70 seconds. Stir until smooth and then pour over 5 cups of the cereal; stir until cereal is coated. Place in a greased 9 x 13-inch glass dish. Sprinkle 2 cups miniature marshmallows on top of cereal mixture. Carefully pour caramel mixture over marshmallows; refrigerate to set up. Repeat second layer of rice cereal mixture, using the rest of the butter, marshmallows, and cereal. Place second layer of Rice Krispies mixture on top of caramel layer; chill until firm. Makes 12 to 15 servings.

CARAMEL
1 (14-oz.) bag caramels, unwrapped
1 (14-oz.) can sweetened condensed milk
1 stick butter

RICE KRISPIES
1 1/2 sticks butter, divided
10 cups miniature marshmallows, divided
10 cups Rice Krispies, divided

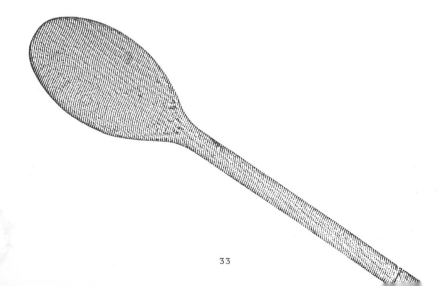

BANANA BANANA BAR

2 1/2 cups flour
1 2/3 cups sugar
1 1/4 tsp. baking powder
1 1/2 tsp. baking soda
1 1/2 sticks butter, softened
2/3 cup buttermilk
2 cups mashed banana
2 eggs

FROSTING

4 cups powdered sugar
1 stick butter, softened
2 tsp. vanilla
Enough cream to make
    spreadable

Stir the four dry ingredients together. Add butter, buttermilk, and banana; beat until flour is moist. Add eggs and beat 2 additional minutes.

Grease a 15 x 10-inch jellyroll pan and pour batter into it. Bake at 350 degrees for 30 to 35 minutes; let cool.

To make the frosting, beat the first three ingredients together until smooth. Add enough cream to make a spreadable consistency; frost cooled bars. Makes 16 to 20 servings.

PUMPKIN DESSERT BAR

Mix the first seven ingredients as you would for pumpkin pie, pouring batter into a greased 9 x 13-inch glass dish. Sprinkle cake mix over the top and then drizzle with butter. Sprinkle with pecans if using. Bake at 350 degrees for 45 to 55 minutes. Makes 12 to 15 servings.

2 (15-oz.) cans pumpkin
4 eggs
1 1/3 cups sugar
1 (12-oz.) can evaporated
  milk
2 tsp. cinnamon
1 tsp. nutmeg
1/2 tsp. ginger
1 yellow cake mix
2 sticks butter, melted
1 cup chopped pecans
  (optional)

LACE COOKIES

Stir the first four ingredients together. Add the egg and then the remaining ingredients; stir until combined. Line baking sheet with parchment paper. Use a teaspoon of batter for each cookie, allowing room between cookies, as they spread when baked. Bake at 325 degrees for 8 to 10 minutes, or until golden brown. Cool completely before trying to remove from paper. Very fragile, but wonderful! Makes about 5 dozen cookies.

1 cup uncooked
  quick-cooking oats
1 cup sugar
1 stick butter, melted
2 1/2 tbsp. flour
1 egg, beaten
1/4 tsp. salt
2 tsp. vanilla extract

SUGAR COOKIES

2 cups sugar
1 cup butter
2 eggs
1 cup vegetable oil
5 cups flour
2 tsp. baking soda
2 tsp. cream of tartar
1/4 tsp. salt
2 tsp. vanilla
Sugar

Cream sugar and butter together and then add eggs one at a time, and then add vegetable oil. Mix all dry ingredients together and then gradually add to batter; add vanilla and then chill. Form into 1-inch dough balls and then roll in sugar. Press down and mark with fork tines. Bake at 350 degrees for 8 to 10 minutes. Makes 4 to 5 dozen.

CHOCOLATE CHIP COOKIES

1/2 cup shortening
1 stick butter, softened
3/4 cup sugar
3/4 cup light brown sugar
2 eggs
2 1/4 cups flour
1 tsp. baking soda
1 tsp. salt
1 tsp. vanilla extract
2 1/4 cups semisweet chocolate chips

Using an electric stand mixer, cream first four ingredients together until creamy. Add eggs and beat 1 minute. Add flour, baking soda, and salt. Add vanilla and then stir in chocolate chips. Chill for 10 minutes in refrigerator.

Using an ice cream scoop, drop dough onto two parchment paper–lined baking sheets, placing 6 on each tray. Bake at 350 degrees for 10 to 12 minutes, or until edges are brown; let cool. Makes 12 large cookies.

Toffee Cookies: Increase flour by 1/2 cup, and stir in 2 cups toffee bits instead of chocolate chips.

GINGERSNAP COOKIES

Cream shortening, sugar, and molasses
together. Add egg, baking soda, salt, and
spices; mix until well blended. Add flour
and mix until combined; chill.

    Roll dough into 1-inch balls and then roll
in sugar. Place 2 inches apart on a parchment paper–lined baking sheet. Flatten
slightly with fingers. Bake at 350 degrees
for 6 to 8 minutes, or until cookies appear
slightly cracked. Makes 4 to 5 dozen.

3/4 cup shortening
1 cup light brown sugar
1/4 cup molasses
1 egg
2 tsp. baking soda
1/2 tsp. salt
2 tsp. cinnamon
2 tsp. ground ginger
1 tsp. cloves
2 cups flour
Sugar

NOTES

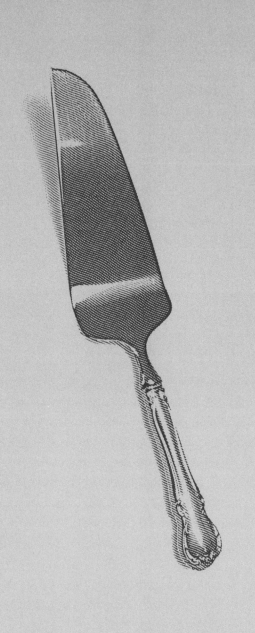

———— desserts ————

By the third year, we had finally reached a plateau in Sue's home. Health department regulations, visibility, and space limited any expansion. I kept envisioning some type of bakery/cafe but could not imagine that a reality. In July 1995, my former husband, Tom Wolf, purchased the Hesse Building specifically for our bake shop, and encouraged—no forced— Sue and I, ready or not, into the restaurant business.

The Hesse Building, a three-story Italianate, was built in 1869 and was home to B. B. Hesse & Sons Clothiers for over 100 years. The building, empty for six years, had fallen to disrepair. Restoration of the building itself excited the whole town of Fort Madison.

Tom oversaw the renovation of the building to its former grandeur. The old oak display cabinets that formerly held slacks and shirts now hold recipe books, serving pieces, and assorted antique cake stands. The punched tin ceiling was painted. Incredible light fixtures were removed to be repainted, only to reveal original collars of brass. Dressing room mirrors were reconfigured and added to shelving to create a spectacular backdrop. The windows, bricked shut for years, were opened while the old wooden floor, relieved of linoleum, was restored.

Sue and I visited cafes and bakeries in Iowa, Mississippi, Colorado, and California. We paid close attention to menu offerings, service area efficiency, and customer ease of ordering. Gracious proprietors allowed us to tour their kitchens where we discovered the importance of equipment layout and its direct link to bottom-line success of the business. We organized our families in recipe research and testing as well as exploring additional bakeries and cafes.

We developed a vision of our restaurant, but we needed to balance that concept with the reality of successful entrepreneurship. Despite the many innovative ideas gathered from other places, we recognized the need to focus on a restaurant that would be successful in Fort Madison, Iowa. Armed with an overwhelming supply of information, we still believed, perhaps foolishly, we could be successful at the Ivy.

We worked diligently on a business plan—an attempt to predict the future. Some of our predictions were accurate and some we missed. We learned we couldn't always count on life going along as outlined, so at the Bake Shoppe, we adhered to the philosophy, "Because life is always uncertain, feel free to eat dessert first!"

NEW YORK–STYLE CHEESECAKE

Mix all crust ingredients together and pat into the bottom and up the sides of a well-greased 10-inch springform pan. Bake at 350 degrees for 10 minutes, or until fragrant; set aside.

For the filling, use an electric mixer to beat the cream cheese, mascarpone, and sugar together. Continue beating, wiping down sides two or three times, until light and smooth, about 10 minutes. Add eggs, one at a time, mixing just until incorporated; add vanilla. Pour filling into crust and then place pan in a water bath. Bake at 350 degrees for 45 minutes. Reduce heat and bake at 250 degrees for another 45 minutes. Turn oven off and, with door ajar, let cheesecake sit in oven for 45 minutes. Move to the counter and cool another 45 minutes. Refrigerate at least 8 hours before serving. Makes 12 to 16 servings.

CRUST

2 ¼ cups graham cracker crumbs
¾ stick butter, melted
4 ½ tbsp. sugar

FILLING

4 8-oz. pkg. cream cheese, room temperature
8 oz. mascarpone cheese, room temperature
1 ½ cups sugar
6 eggs, at room temperature
1 ½ tsp. vanilla

PUMPKIN CHEESECAKE

CRUST

2 ¼ cups crushed
   gingersnap cookies
½ stick butter, melted

FILLING

3 8-oz. pkg. cream cheese,
   room temperature
8 oz. mascarpone cheese,
   room temperature
1 ½ cups sugar
6 eggs, room temperature
1 (15-oz.) can pumpkin
1 tsp. vanilla extract
2 tsp. cinnamon
1 tsp. ground cloves

For the crust, mix the cookie crumbs and butter together. Pour into a well-greased 10-inch springform pan. Pat crust into the bottom and up the sides of pan. Bake at 350 degrees until golden, about 10 minutes; set aside.

For the filling, beat the cream cheese, mascarpone cheese, and sugar together with an electric mixer until smooth and totally combined, scraping sides occasionally. Add the eggs one at a time, and mix just until incorporated. Stir in the pumpkin and spices.

Pour filling into crust and then place pan in a water bath. Bake at 350 degrees for 50 minutes. Reduce heat and bake at 250 degrees for 45 minutes. Turn off oven and, with door ajar, let cheesecake sit in oven for about 1 hour. Refrigerate overnight, allowing time to set up before serving. Makes 12 to 16 servings.

PINEAPPLE TORTE

Cream butter and ½ cup sugar together.
Gradually add egg yolks and beat until
combined. Combine flour, salt, and baking
powder and mix into the batter alternately
with milk. Pour into two greased and
parchment paper–lined 8-inch round cake
pans. It will be very little batter. Bake at 350
degrees for 15 minutes. While cakes are baking,
whip egg whites until soft peaks form and
then gradually add remaining sugar. Beat
until stiff peaks form and then add vanilla.
Spread meringue on top of baked cake layers.
Sprinkle with pecans and return to oven for
15 minutes at 325 degrees; set aside to cool.

Make the filling by whipping cream and
then folding in remaining ingredients.

To assemble, place the first cake layer on
a serving piece with meringue side down.
Spread the filling on top. Place second cake
layer with the meringue side up. This is a
beautiful dessert and it tastes great as well.
Makes 8 to 12 servings.

1 stick butter
1 ¼ cups sugar, divided
4 egg yolks, well beaten
⅔ cup flour
¼ tsp. salt
1 tsp. baking powder
¼ cup milk
4 egg whites
1 tsp. vanilla extract
¾ cup toasted pecans

FILLING

1 cup heavy whipping
  cream
1 ½ tbsp. powdered sugar
1 cup crushed pineapple,
  drained
½ tsp. vanilla extract

PEACH COBBLER

PASTRY

1 cup flour
¼ tsp. salt
½ cup shortening
3 tbsp. ice water

FILLING

½ cup butter
9 ripe peaches, peeled
   and sliced
1 ½ cups water
1 ½ cups sugar, divided
2 tbsp. flour
Dash of cinnamon
Pinch of salt

To make the pastry, combine the first three ingredients with a pastry blender; add ice water and form dough. Wrap in wax paper and chill 30 minutes. Roll out dough and cut into $1/4$- to $1/2$-inch strips. Reserve enough strips to lattice top of cobbler. Place remaining strips on a baking sheet and bake at 450 degrees for 10 minutes, or until crisp.

For the filling, mix the first three ingredients together in a saucepan and let come to a boil. Reserve 2 tablespoons sugar for top of cobbler and then stir remaining sugar, flour, cinnamon, and salt into boiling mixture until dissolved.

Grease an 8 x 8-inch baking dish. Place half of the peach mixture into the dish; top with cooked pastry strips. Add the remaining peach mixture and lace uncooked pastry strips over the top; sprinkle with reserved sugar. Bake at 375 degrees for 35 to 40 minutes. Delicious served warm with cream. Makes 8 servings.

JUDY'S FRUIT PIZZA

Cream first three ingredients together until light and fluffy. Add next five ingredients, mixing well. Pat into a greased 15 x 10-inch jellyroll pan. Bake at 400 degrees for 10 minutes; set aside to cool.

For the filling, beat the cream cheese, remaining sugar, and fruit juice together until no lumps remain and filling is smooth. Spread filling on cooled crust. Slice assorted fruits and place on top of filling; chill. We drizzle Chocolate Topping (see page 28) over the pizza as a garnish. Makes 12 to 16 servings.

½ cup shortening
1 stick butter, softened
1 ½ cups sugar
2 eggs
2 tsp. cream of tartar
1 tsp. baking soda
1 tsp. vanilla extract
2 ¾ cups flour

FILLING

1 ½ pkg. cream cheese,
   room temperature
   (12 oz. total)
½ cup sugar
2 tbsp. orange or
   pineapple juice
Assorted fruits

TIRAMISU

½ cup espresso or strong coffee

½ tsp. sugar

3 tbsp. Kahlua or other coffee liqueur

24 hard ladyfingers

5 eggs, separated

1 tbsp. coffee liqueur

½ cup sugar

⅔ cup powdered sugar

24 oz. mascarpone cheese, room temperature

1 heaping tbsp. sugar

3 oz. grated semisweet chocolate, divided

1 ½ cups whipping cream

3 tbsp. Kahlua

Combine espresso and $1/2$ teaspoon sugar. Boil over medium heat for 1 minute. Remove from heat, and stir in 3 tablespoons Kahlua or coffee liqueur; cool completely. Line a 9 x 13-inch glass dish with ladyfingers. Drizzle with half of the cooled coffee mixture.

Beat egg yolks, 1 tablespoon coffee liqueur, and $1/2$ cup sugar for 2 minutes. Add powdered sugar and mascarpone cheese, beating until smooth.

Beat egg whites with 1 heaping tablespoon sugar until stiff peaks form. Gently fold into mascarpone mixture.

Spread half of the mixture on top of ladyfingers. Sprinkle with one-third of the semisweet chocolate. Repeat layers, ending with another third of the chocolate.

Beat whipping cream until soft peaks form. Fold in Kahlua and then spread on top. Sprinkle remaining chocolate over cream as a garnish. Refrigerate for at least 8 hours. Makes 12 to 16 servings.

CHOCOLATE BREAD PUDDING WITH WHITE CHOCOLATE SAUCE

Preheat oven 325 degrees. Bring cream, 1 cup sugar, and milk to a simmer in a heavy saucepan, stirring until sugar dissolves; remove from heat. Add 2 cups chocolate chips and whisk until melted and smooth. Whisk eggs and vanilla in a large bowl to blend. Gradually whisk in hot chocolate mixture. Cool custard for 10 minutes, stirring often.

Add bread cubes and remaining chocolate chips to custard and toss to coat. Transfer to a 9 x 13-inch greased dish. Sprinkle 4 tablespoons sugar over mixture. Bake until custard thickens and center is just set, about 40 to 45 minutes. Serve warm with White Chocolate Sauce.

For the sauce, heat cream just until bubbles form around edge of pan, but not to boiling. Remove from heat and then whisk in white chocolate chips and stir until melted and smooth. Makes 12 to 15 servings.

3 ½ cups whipping cream
1 cup sugar
½ cup milk
2 ½ cups semisweet
  chocolate chips, divided
2 eggs
2 tsp. vanilla extract
8 cups French bread, cut
  in 1-inch cubes
4 tbsp. sugar

WHITE CHOCOLATE SAUCE
1 ½ cups heavy cream
1 cup white
  chocolate chips

DECADENT CHOCOLATE TORTE

½ cup butter
½ cup light corn syrup
1 cup semisweet
  chocolate chips
½ cup light brown sugar
3 eggs
1 tsp. vanilla extract
1 cup flour
1 cup chopped walnuts

GLAZE
1 ⅓ cups semisweet
  chocolate chips
1 cup heavy cream

Butter and flour a 9-inch-round cake pan. In a saucepan, heat butter and corn syrup together until butter is melted; stir in chocolate chips until melted and smooth. Add sugar and eggs, and then stir until well blended. Stir in vanilla, flour, and nuts. Pour batter into pan and bake at 350 degrees for 30 minutes. Cool in pan for 10 minutes and then turn cake out on a rack.

For the glaze, put chocolate chips in a heatproof bowl. Bring the cream to a boil in a saucepan. Pour the cream over the chocolate and gently whisk until all the chocolate is melted and smooth. If it is too thick, thin with more cream, 1 tablespoon at a time.

Place a piece of wax paper under the cake and rack. Pour the warm glaze over the cake and spread it with a spatula over the top and sides. Let is set for about 1 hour before transferring to a cake plate or serving dish. Makes 6 to 8 servings.

FUDGE MUFFINS

Melt butter and chocolate in a large bowl
in the microwave for 90 seconds or until
smooth. Beat in sugar, salt, and flour. Add
eggs one at a time, stirring in but not beating;
add vanilla and nuts. Line muffin pans with
paper liners and fill each about two-thirds full.
Bake at 325 degrees for 25 minutes. Do not
overbake. Makes 24 muffins.

2 sticks butter, melted
⅔ cup semisweet
   chocolate chips
1 ¾ cups sugar
Pinch of salt
1 cup flour
4 eggs
1 tsp. vanilla extract
2 cups chopped pecans

CHOCOLATE SAUCE

Heat sugar and cream together in a saucepan. In a separate pan, melt chocolate and
butter together. Combine two mixtures
and boil for 3 minutes, stirring constantly;
add vanilla. Serve drizzled over ice cream,
profiteroles, or cheesecake. Makes about 1 cup.

½ cup sugar
¾ cup heavy cream
1 square unsweetened
   chocolate (1 oz.)
1 tbsp. butter
1 tsp. vanilla

DOROTHY'S BLACKBOTTOM CUPCAKES

1 (8-oz.) pkg. cream cheese
1 egg
⅓ cup sugar
⅛ tsp. salt
1 cup semisweet
  chocolate chips
1 ½ cups flour
1 cup sugar
¼ cup cocoa
1 tsp. baking soda
½ tsp. salt
1 cup water
⅓ cup vegetable oil
1 tbsp. vinegar
1 tsp. vanilla extract
¼ cup sugar
¼ cup sliced almonds

Beat cream cheese, egg, $^1/_3$ cup sugar, and $^1/_8$ teaspoon salt together until light and fluffy. Stir in chocolate chips; set aside.

Sift flour, 1 cup sugar, cocoa, baking soda, and $^1/_2$ teaspoon salt together. Add water, oil, vinegar, and vanilla, and then beat thoroughly.

Line muffin pans with paper liners. Fill cups about one-third full and then top each with a heaping teaspoon of cream cheese mixture. Combine $^1/_4$ cup sugar and almonds in a bowl and then sprinkle on top of cupcakes. Bake at 325 degrees for 20 to 25 minutes. Makes 24 cupcakes.

NOTES

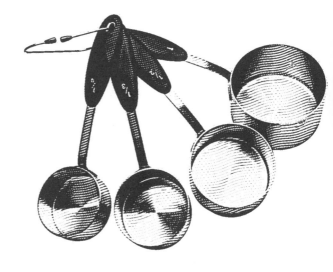

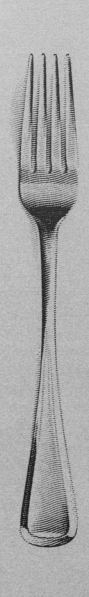

—————— entrees ——————

The first year at the Ivy Bake Shoppe and Cafe in downtown Fort Madison was a blur. Because we were afraid an overwhelming crowd of people would appear at our grand opening and expect good food, we quietly unlocked the door on Monday morning, November 5, 1995, after a Sunday night health department inspection and approval. Surprisingly, throngs of people expecting good food in a warm friendly atmosphere appeared. They received just what they expected.

We survived each day and returned each morning ready for challenges and thrilled with the stories of the previous day. Luckily, we had hired an experienced cook, Linda Reeves, and she guided us through the first harrowing weeks. Though we lacked experience, our enthusiasm made up for our short-comings. It was amazingly rewarding to see people embrace our concept of a bakery and cafe in Fort Madison, Iowa!

At first, the chalkboard menu was very limited. We offered our Meat and Vegetable Quiche, as well as Ham, Turkey, Roast Beef, or Chicken Salad sandwiches. We served two soup choices, and the "Special of the Day." There were usually five different side salad choices, including Cottage Cheese, Vegetable Medley, Broccoli Salad, Kitty's Pasta, and Green Bean Artichoke Salad.

As we became more organized, established routines, and grew more comfortable in our new surroundings, we were able to expand the menu. Now we have trouble limiting what we write on the chalkboard because everyone has their favorites. The following recipes are some of our "specials" of the day and favorites of customers as well as staff.

CHICKEN AND SPINACH LASAGNA

1 ½ sticks butter

¾ cup flour

6 cups milk, heated

1 ½ tsp. dried basil

1 ½ tsp. dried oregano

1 tsp. garlic powder or
   1 clove garlic, minced

1 ¾ cups cottage cheese

1 tbsp. white wine

1 tsp. Tabasco sauce

1 tbsp. dried oregano

1 tbsp. dried basil

2 eggs, slightly beaten

15 to 20 Lasagna noodles,
   cooked or no-boil

2 ½ lb. cut-up cooked
   chicken (a rotisserie
   chicken works well and
   saves time)

¾ lb. spinach

½ lb. fresh mushrooms,
   sliced

1 ½ cups grated
   mozzarella cheese

½ cup grated Parmesan
   cheese (for top only)

Melt butter in a saucepan over medium-low heat. Add flour and stir until smooth, cooking another minute or so. Slowly add warmed milk and stir until sauce becomes thick and bubbly, about 4 to 5 minutes. Stir in seasonings and then set aside.

Stir the cottage cheese, wine, tabasco, 1 tablespoon oregano, 1 tablespoon basil, and eggs together in a bowl, mixing until thoroughly combined.

Grease a 10 x 15-inch pan or a lasagna pan at least 2 inches deep. Put some of the white sauce on the bottom of the pan. Place a layer of noodles over the sauce and then add more sauce. Layer, in order, using one-third of each: chicken, spinach, mushrooms, cottage cheese mixture, and mozzarella. Top with lasagna noodles and sauce and repeat layers two more times. Top last layer with Parmesan cheese.

Spray foil and cover pan carefully. Bake at 350 degrees for 45 minutes. Remove foil and bake an additional 15 minutes, or until nicely browned on top. After removing from oven, let sit 10 minutes before serving. Makes 10 to 12 generous portions.

CHICKEN JERUSALEM

Dredge chicken in flour and then brown in butter and olive oil in a frying pan over medium-high heat; drain.

Grease a 9 x 13-inch glass pan and place chicken in bottom. Layer mushrooms and artichoke hearts over chicken. In a bowl, mix remaining ingredients and then pour over chicken mixture. Cover and bake at 350 degrees for 1 1/2 hours. Makes 8 servings.

1 1/2 lb. chicken breasts, cut in pieces
Flour
2 tbsp. butter
2 tbsp. olive oil
1 lb. mushrooms, thinly sliced
2 cups artichoke hearts, cut in half
3 cloves garlic, chopped
1/2 tsp. dried oregano
1 tsp. coarsely ground black pepper
2 cups tomato wedges

CHICKEN ENCHILADAS

3 cups cooked,
chopped chicken
1 potato, peeled,
shredded, and rinsed
under cold water
¾ cup diced onion
¾ cup diced green
bell pepper
1 cup sour cream
1 ½ tsp. ground pepper
1 can cream of chicken
soup, condensed
12 (10-in.) flour tortillas
Salsa or enchilada sauce
Grated Monterey Jack and
cheddar cheese

Mix the first seven ingredients together until well combined. Lay a tortilla on the counter, and place an ice cream scoop of chicken mixture in the middle. Roll up, spreading the filling the length of the tortilla. Place on a greased baking sheet seam side down. Repeat with remaining ingredients. You may freeze the enchiladas at this point. When ready to serve, place enchiladas on a greased baking sheet and pour enchilada sauce or salsa over top to cover. Generously sprinkle with Monterey Jack and cheddar cheese. Bake at 400 degrees for 20 minutes. Serve with a dollop of sour cream and extra salsa. Makes 8 to 12 servings.

CHICKEN ALMONDINE

In a medium saucepan, combine the mayonnaise, flour, onion, and garlic salt. Gradually add the milk and cook over low heat, stirring constantly until mixture thickens. Add cheese and wine and stir until cheese melts. Remove from heat.

In a large bowl, combine the mayonnaise mixture, spaghetti, chicken, broccoli, half of the almonds, the mushrooms and pimientos; toss lightly. Pour into a greased 9 x 13-inch dish. Top with remaining almonds. Bake at 350 degrees for 40 minutes, or until thoroughly heated. Makes 10 to 12 servings.

¾ cup mayonnaise
⅓ cup flour
2 tbsp. minced onion
1 tsp. garlic salt
2 ¼ cups milk, warmed
1 cup grated Swiss cheese
⅓ cup dry white wine
12 oz. spaghetti, cooked and drained
3 cups chopped, cooked chicken
4 cups broccoli, cut in bite-size pieces
1 ½ cups sliced almonds, divided
4 oz. sliced mushrooms
¼ cup pimientos

CHICKEN POTPIE

¼ cup butter
½ cup flour
2 cups heavy cream
2 cups chicken broth
1 ½ tsp. salt
½ tsp. ground pepper
3 lb. cooked, cut up
   chicken (a deli rotisserie
   chicken works well)
1 lb. mushrooms,
   thinly sliced
Piecrusts (1 for bottom
   12 x 10; 1 for top 9 x 13)
1 tbsp. butter, melted

Melt $^1/_4$ cup butter in a heavy saucepan over low heat. Add the flour and stir until smooth. Cook 1 minute while stirring constantly. Heat the cream in the microwave for 1 minute and then gradually add to saucepan. Cooking over medium heat, gradually add the chicken broth as mixture thickens until all has been added. Sauce should be thick and bubbly. Stir in salt, pepper, chicken, and mushrooms. Place 1 piecrust in bottom of pan. Pour mixture into the pastry-lined 9 x 13-inch dish. Place remaining crust on top of pie. Fold edges together. Cut three or four slits in top for steam to escape. Brush 1 tablespoon melted butter over top of crust. Bake at 400 degrees for 30 to 35 minutes. Makes 8 to 10 servings.

MEAT OR VEGETABLE QUICHE

Place assorted diced or chopped vegetables (carrots, mushrooms, broccoli, spinach, diced tomatoes, etc.) or meat (crumbled bacon, sliced ham, crumbled sausage) in a greased 9-inch pie pan. In a food processor, combine eggs, cottage cheese, flour, baking soda, and salt and then process until smooth, about 1 to 2 minutes. Add melted butter and cheese and continue processing. Slowly pour mixture over vegetables or meat. Do not overfill. Bake at 375 degrees for 15 minutes. Reduce heat to 325 degrees, and continue cooking for 20 to 25 minutes more. Makes 6 servings.

Assorted vegetables
  or meat
5 eggs
1 ¼ cups cottage cheese
½ cup flour
¾ tsp. baking soda
½ tsp. salt
3 tbsp. butter,
  slightly melted
1 cup grated Monterey
  Jack cheese

GREEK PIZZA

Spread 2 tablespoons tomato sauce on top of a pita bread round. Top with spinach, olives, tomatoes, feta cheese, red onion rings, parsley, and garlic. Sprinkle mozzarella cheese over top. Place in an oven preheated to 425 degrees directly on the rack. Bake for 5 minutes. Serves as many as you make.

Tomato sauce with
  basil and oregano
Pita rounds
Spinach
Sliced black olives
Tomatoes, diced
Feta cheese, crumbled
Red onion, sliced thin
  in rings
Chopped parsley
Chopped garlic
Grated mozzarella cheese

COLD CHICKEN LINGUINE

1 lb. linguine noodles,
  cooked according to
  package directions
½ cup pine nuts, toasted in
  1 tbsp. butter
½ cup chicken broth
6 chicken breasts,
  baked and cut in
  bite-size pieces
1 (15-oz.) can garbanzo
  beans, drained
2 (6-oz.) jars marinated
  artichoke hearts, chopped
1 cup blanched snow peas
8 oz. mushrooms, sliced
1 (20-oz.) jar stuffed olives,
  drained and sliced
1 (20-oz.) can pitted black
  olives, sliced
1 red bell pepper,
  cut into strips
½ cup olive oil
3 tbsp. red wine vinegar
¼ cup chopped parsley
2 tbsp. Dijon mustard
½ tsp. curry powder
1 tsp. garlic powder
Salt and pepper to taste

Combine all the ingredients in a large bowl. Refrigerate for several hours before serving. Flavor improves if salad is refrigerated overnight. Makes 20 to 25 servings.

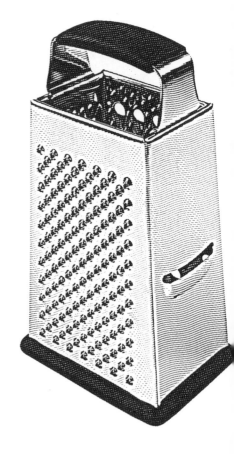

THE IVY'S NOODLES

Add the first three ingredients in a stand
mixer and then beat in milk. Begin adding
flour until the dough is moist but not sticky;
turn out and gather together. When you roll
it out, dip dough in flour lightly. Process
with a pasta machine. We freeze our noodles,
and then package them. We keep them in
the freezer for up to 3 months until ready
to use. Makes 1 1/2 pounds.

11 egg yolks
1 tsp. baking powder
1 tsp. salt
1 tbsp. milk
2 cups flour

VARIATION: SPINACH NOODLES

Omit the milk and add 1 1/2 cups dry spinach,
pulsed for 5 seconds in a food processor.
It will take 3 to 4 cups flour for spinach
noodles, as they are stickier because of the
liquid in the spinach. Process and freeze the
same as above.

PASTA PRIMAVERA

1 medium onion, chopped
5 cloves garlic, chopped
½ cup olive oil
2 tsp. salt
1 tbsp. dried basil
1 tbsp. dried oregano
1 ½ cups flour
2 ½ cups milk, warmed
½ lb. spinach noodles
½ lb. white noodles
2 cups broccoli florets
2 cups cauliflower florets
½ red bell pepper,
  slivered in strips
Grated Parmesan cheese

Saute onion and garlic over medium heat with oil until onion is soft. Add rest of seasonings, stirring to fully combine. Add the flour and stir until heated. Add the milk, whisking constantly, and continue cooking until the sauce is thick and bubbly; set aside.

In a separate pan, add spinach noodles and white noodles to 2 quarts of boiling water. Cook for about 5 minutes and then add broccoli and cauliflower; stir often. Cook for 5 minutes more and then remove from stove and drain very well, but do not rinse. Stir in bell pepper slivers. Add sauce and gently stir to combine and cover pasta. Pour into an oven-safe bowl and sprinkle with Parmesan cheese. Set under broiler just to melt cheese, about 1 to 2 minutes; serve. Makes 4 to 6 servings.

Variation: Add pieces of grilled or rotisserie chicken to the pasta before adding the sauce.

BEEF STROGANOFF

Combine the flour and salt and then dredge the meat in the mixture. Heat butter in a skillet over medium-high heat and brown meat quickly, turning to sear all sides. Reduce heat and add mushrooms, onion, and garlic. Cook 3 to 4 minutes, or until onion is translucent; remove meat mixture.

To make the sauce, use the same skillet with pan drippings, and add the butter. Blend in flour and then add tomato paste, stirring continually to ensure mixture does not boil. Slowly pour in cold broth and continue stirring until mixture thickens. No lumps!

Return meat mixture to skillet. Stir in sour cream and sherry; heat through. Makes 4 servings.

1 tbsp. flour
½ tsp. salt
1 ½ lb. sirloin,
    cut in ¼-in. strips
2 tbsp. butter
8 oz. mushrooms,
    thinly sliced
½ cup chopped onion
1 clove garlic, minced

SAUCE
2 tbsp. butter
4 tbsp. flour
1 tbsp. tomato paste
1 ¼ cups beef broth
1 cup sour cream
2 tbsp. sherry

ELINOR'S MEAT LOAF

1 ½ lb. ground beef
½ lb. ground pork
1 egg, beaten
1 cup chopped onion
1 cup dried breadcrumbs
1 ½ cups milk
1 ¼ tsp. salt
¼ tsp. pepper
2 tbsp. dried leaf sage
¼ tsp. celery seed

In a bowl, mix all ingredients together, incorporating thoroughly. Place in a greased loaf pan. Bake at 350 degrees for 1 ½ to 2 hours. Makes 8 servings.

SPAGHETTI SAUCE

3 (4-oz.) cans tomato paste
1 quart water
¾ tsp. dried marjoram
2 tbsp. sugar
2 tbsp. salt
¾ tsp. cayenne pepper
3 whole red chile peppers
4 oz. mushrooms, sliced
3 cloves garlic, minced
½ cup grated onion
½ tsp. chili powder
3 bay leaves
½ cup sliced black olives
3 lb. ground round
  hamburger
2 tbsp. butter
⅓ cup flour

Place the first thirteen ingredients in a large pan and simmer slowly for 1 hour, stirring occasionally. While this is simmering, brown hamburger in the butter. After browning, add flour to meat and stir thoroughly to absorb liquid. Remove bay leaves and whole peppers from sauce and then add meat. Cook over very low heat for another 1 ½ hours. Stir occasionally to be sure the sauce isn't sticking. Serve over pasta. Makes 12 servings.

CHINESE PORK WRAP

To make the wrap, spread a tortilla with Peanut Sauce. Lay 3 or 4 pieces of tenderloin on lower third of tortilla. Layer rest of ingredients on top. Roll tight and cut in half to serve.

    To make peanut sauce, stir ingredients together in a saucepan until well combined. Stir constantly, bringing to a boil for 1 minute. Remove from heat and continue stirring 1 minute more. Makes 6 to 8 servings.

8 (10-in.) tortillas

¾ to 1 ¼ lb. pork tenderloin, cooked and sliced thin

1 (8-oz.) small can bamboo shoots, drained

1 (8-oz.) can water chestnuts, drained and chopped

1 (14.5-oz.) can bean sprouts, drained

2 cups snow peas, blanched and cut in thirds

½ head green cabbage, shredded

⅓ head purple cabbage, shredded

4 carrots, peeled and julienned

PEANUT SAUCE

½ cup chicken broth

2 tbsp. hoisin sauce

2 tbsp. sesame oil

2 tbsp. soy sauce

2 tbsp. peanut butter

1 tsp. cornstarch

HAM, PECAN, AND BLUE CHEESE PASTA

1 ¼ lb. ham, cut into
  bite-size strips
2 cups toasted pecans
6 oz. blue cheese,
  crumbled
¾ cup snipped parsley
½ cup olive oil
4 tbsp. fresh rosemary,
  or 1 tsp. dried
2 cloves garlic, minced
1 tsp. coarse black pepper
1 lb. cooked bow-tie pasta

Combine all ingredients except pasta in a large mixing bowl. Cover and let stand at room temperature for 30 minutes. Cook pasta per package directions. Drain pasta, rinse with cold water, and drain again. Add pasta to the mixture and toss to serve. Serve over lettuce leaves. Makes 6 to 8 servings.

PORK TENDERLOIN

2 tbsp. vegetable oil
2 tbsp. soy sauce
2 tbsp. hoisin sauce
1 ½ tsp. sugar
1 (¾- to 1 ¼-lb.)
  pork tenderloin

Combine oil, soy sauce, hoisin sauce, and sugar together. Marinate tenderloin in mixture for at least 30 minutes and up to 24 hours. Preheat oven to 500 degrees. Cover baking sheet with foil. Place tenderloin on a rack on a baking sheet. Bake 10 minutes on each side, or until internal temperature is 160 degrees. Delicious and tender! Makes 4 to 5 servings.

TURKEY MELON WRAP

Cut rind from cantaloupe and discard; slice cantaloupe into strips. Mix mayonnaise and horseradish together, and spread tortillas with some of the mixture. Top mixture with a lettuce leaf, then layer turkey, cheese, and cantaloupe slices. Roll up jellyroll fashion. Cut in half and serve. Makes 6 to 10 servings.

½ cantaloupe
1 cup mayonnaise
3 tsp. horseradish
6 to 10 (10-in.) tortillas
Lettuce leaves
1 lb. sliced turkey
1 cup grated Monterey Jack cheese

GRILLED CHEESE WITH VEGGIES

Combine first three ingredients in a stand mixer; beat until smooth. Add next two ingredients, and stir thoroughly. Spread one-sixth of the mixture on pita bread and place under broiler for 1 minute or until cheese bubbles; remove. Blanch a handful of vegetables in boiling water for 1 minute. Drain and then add to ½ side of pita and then close pita, securing with a toothpick, and serve. Makes 4 to 6 servings.

6 oz. cheddar cheese, grated
3 oz. Monterey Jack cheese, grated
½ cup mayonnaise
1 tsp. dry mustard
2 tbsp. Tabasco sauce
6 pita rounds
1 qt. assorted vegetables (broccoli, cauliflower, snow peas, julienned carrots, etc.)

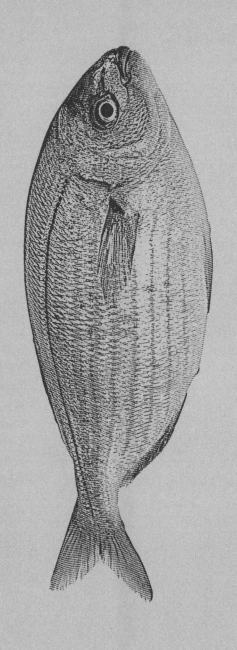

—— fish & seafood ——

"The rest is history," "Change is good," and "Watch out
what you wish for," all applied to the Bake Shoppe over
the next couple of years. We outgrew our space
immediately and, in April of 1996, added a successful
screened-in porch. People enjoyed sitting on the porch,
watching the barges navigate the mighty Mississippi while
sipping their cappuccino or enjoying an Ivy-baked treat.

By fall, our concern about winter seating for the "porch"
people grew. Timing was on our side. The basket shop adjacent
to the bakery decided to relocate. Tom came to our rescue
again. French doors he salvaged were installed, creating an
additional dining room in November 1996.

By then the *Des Moines Register* had announced that the
Register's Annual Great Bike Ride Across Iowa (RAGBRAI)
was going to end in Fort Madison in July of the next year.
We immediately started making plans to feed as many of the
10,000 bicyclists and their 15,000 support staff as we could
get in the building.

As they began arriving, we realized we were grossly under-
prepared. We ran out of meats and cheeses and, out of neces-
sity, created our now famous Vegetable Sandwich—fresh vegetables
served with our pesto mayonnaise. It was all we had left!

RAGBRAI marked the beginning of our belief and confi-
dence in ourselves. It empowered our staff—they recognized
their abilities to manage the unexpected. Our focus to serve the
finest food in a warm and nurturing atmosphere defined us,
and it worked. Word-of-mouth advertising brought customers

from all over the area. We had developed a base of local
regulars, but the restaurant soon gained customers from all
over the United States.

In retrospect, it is easy to see how naïve we were in the restaurant business. We realized the success of a business isn't always
about the business itself. Sometimes it is about the soul of the
business. Sue and I always relied on a higher power to guide
us and always remained hopeful that "something good comes
out of everything."

This chapter contains some great fish and seafood recipes.
You can't be born and raised on the coast of Mississippi without
including a few favorite recipes native to that area. And the Fish
Tacos? This became an Ivy favorite after some California trans-
plants told us they were homesick for San Diego and especially
fish tacos. We invited them into the kitchen and they showed
us how to make them. The first few times, we served them as a
special called California Tacos so people would try them. Now
people ask for them by name.

BARBEQUED SHRIMP

Divide the shrimp equally between two 9 x 13-inch glass pans; set aside. In a saucepan, melt the butter. Add the remaining ingredients and mix thoroughly. Pour heated sauce over all the shrimp and stir to coat. Bake at 400 degrees for 15 to 20 minutes, stirring shrimp after 10 minutes. Shells will be pink when done. Remove shrimp and place in a serving bowl. Ladle the sauce into individual bowls for dipping crusty French bread. Serve with a salad and you'll have a meal that is memorable. Makes 8 servings.

8 lb. shrimp with shells on (21-26 count)
2 lb. butter
½ cup Worcestershire sauce
6 tbsp. coarse ground pepper
2 tsp. ground rosemary
4 lemons, sliced
2 tsp. Tabasco sauce
4 tsp. salt

SHRIMP CAKES WITH REMOULADE SAUCE

3 tbsp. thinly sliced
   green onions
½ cup total minced
   green, yellow,
   and red bell peppers
2 tbsp. vegetable oil
1 lb. small bay shrimp,
   chopped
2 medium zucchini,
   shredded and drained
½ cup heavy cream
1 cup breadcrumbs
3 eggs
Dash of Tabasco sauce
Dash of Worcestershire
   sauce
2 tsp. salt
½ cup grated
   Parmesan cheese
Oil for frying

REMOULADE

½ cup mayonnaise
1 tbsp. brown mustard
3 green onions, thinly sliced
1 clove garlic, crushed
½ tsp. salt
Dash of Tabasco sauce
Dash of Worcestershire
   sauce
1 tsp. lime juice
1 tsp. lime zest

In a large skillet over medium heat, fry onions and bell peppers in oil until almost soft. Add shrimp and cook for 5 minutes. Remove and transfer to a large bowl. Add zucchini, cream, breadcrumbs, and eggs to mixture. Stir well and then add seasonings and cheese.

Heat oil in a skillet over medium heat, covering the bottom. Drop the mixture by tablespoons into hot oil, frying on one side, turning over and frying on the other side until golden brown. Let drain on paper towels and then place in a warm oven until ready to serve.

In a large bowl, blend all remoulade ingredients. Serve with shrimp cakes. Makes 4 to 6 servings.

SUSAN'S SHRIMP AND ARTICHOKE SALAD

Process the dressing ingredients together in a food processor or blender to make a dressing. Marinate shrimp and artichokes in dressing for at least 6 hours or overnight in refrigerator. Use a slotted spoon to remove shrimp and artichokes when ready to serve, and serve with toothpicks. The leftover dressing is also great served over lettuce. Makes 36 appetizers.

DRESSING

½ cup vegetable oil
½ cup olive oil
½ cup white balsamic vinegar
2 tbsp. Dijon mustard
2 tbsp. chopped fresh chives
2 tbsp. minced green onions
½ tsp. salt
½ tsp. sugar
¼ tsp. coarse black pepper

2 lb. cooked, peeled medium shrimp (24-28 count)
2 (15-oz.) cans marinated artichoke hearts, drained and cut in half

SPINACH-STUFFED SALMON

7 oz. fresh spinach leaves
3 oz. cream cheese,
    room temperature
8 oz. mascarpone cheese,
    room temperature
6 (8-oz.) salmon fillets,
    about 1 in. thick
1 cup breadcrumbs
¼ tsp. salt
¼ tsp. pepper
¾ stick butter, melted
½ cup grated Parmesan
    cheese

Pulse spinach in a food processor briefly. Mix spinach with cream cheese and mascarpone cheese. Slice a two-inch slit down the top of each salmon fillet. Fill with spinach mixture. Mix breadcrumbs, salt, pepper, butter, and cheese together and then pat mixture on top of stuffed salmon fillets.

Place on a greased baking sheet skin side down. Bake at 450 degrees for 12 minutes. Makes 6 servings.

HOLLY'S BLACKENED CATFISH CAKES

Mix all fruit salsa ingredients together and allow to sit for 1 hour before serving with the catfish cakes.

Combine the blackening spices in a small bowl. Lightly coat fillets with olive oil and dip into seasoning. Pan cook or broil for 5 minutes on each side; remove and cool.

Flake the fish into a large bowl. Mix in corn, green onions, parsley, eggs, and breadcrumbs; form mixture into 8 large patties (or 24 for appetizers). Heat olive oil and butter in a skillet to medium heat. Cook 5 minutes on each side until crispy. Serve with fruit salsa on the side. Makes 4 servings.

FRUIT SALSA

1 cup freshly chopped fruit
   (pineapple, mango,
   or papaya)
2 tbsp. finely
   chopped cilantro
1 tbsp. finely chopped
   red onion
1 tbsp. lime juice
½ tsp. salt
1 finely diced fresh jalapeño
   (optional)

BLACKENING SPICE

1 tbsp. paprika
1 tsp. cayenne pepper
1 tsp. oregano
1 tsp. salt
1 tsp. fresh ground pepper

5 catfish fillets, (about 2 lb.)
Olive oil
1 fresh ear corn, cooked and
   cut from the cob or ¼ cup
   frozen corn, thawed
2 green onions, thinly
   chopped
¼ cup chopped fresh parsley
3 eggs, slightly beaten
1 ½ cups breadcrumbs
1 tbsp. olive oil
1 tbsp. butter

FISH TACOS

2 avocados, mashed and
blended with the juice of
1 lime
10 to 12 (6-in.) flour
tortillas
2 lb. fried cod fillets or
other white fish,
cut in half
Cabbage, shredded
Grated Monterey Jack
cheese
8 oz. plain yogurt, thinned
with 3 tbsp. sour cream
and the juice of 1 lime
Chopped cilantro
Lime wedges for garnish

Evenly spread mashed avocado down the center of each tortilla. Cut fish in two strips and place in the center of avocado mixture. Layer with cabbage, cheese, and yogurt dressing. Sprinkle with cilantro and serve with lime wedges. Makes 10 to 12 servings.

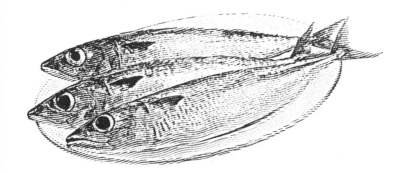

CRAB SALAD

Mix crabmeat with bell pepper, onions, and celery. Mix mayonnaise, lemon juice, and seasonings together and then combine with crab mixture. Adjust seasonings and serve in a hollowed tomato, with a cantaloupe slice, or just by itself over lettuce. Makes 6 to 8 servings.

1 lb. coarsely chopped imitation crabmeat

½ green bell pepper, chopped

3 green onions, white and green parts, chopped

3 ribs celery, chopped

1 cup mayonnaise

Juice of 1 lemon

¼ teaspoon lemon pepper

¼ teaspoon celery salt

NOTES

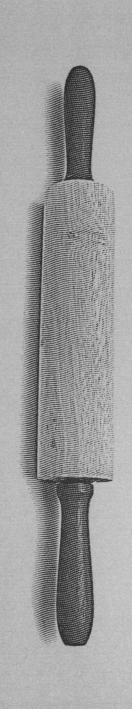

———— cakes & pies ————

Sue and I continued to be blessed with opportunities to expand the Ivy. In 1998, the small piano studio next to our second dining room became available. Instead of adding more seating, we recognized that our bakers needed more space. It was time to invest in some serious commercial equipment.

We updated our business plan and went back to the bank. Sue consoled me as we accepted more debt. "Think of it as a car loan for a really nice car!" she suggested. We then equipped the bakery with a commercial 20-quart mixer, a convection oven and proofer, and lots of counter space. The expansion also allowed us to update the refrigeration and freezer space in the original kitchen.

That same year Sue brought a picture of an apple dessert from one of her fancy catalogs with a high price tag to go with it. She challenged me and our German baker, Renate Butler, to create a similar dessert. After a little bit of this and a little bit of that, the Caramel Apple Tart was born. The spicy apple creation claims honors as the all-time favorite and most requested recipe.

Maybe timing contributes to the demand? The tart slides into the oven at 10:00 a.m., comes out at 10:45 and is drizzled with warm caramel sauce. Perched on a countertop serving pedestal at 11:00 when customers arrive for lunch, the aroma of apples and caramel proves irresistible.

We have been very fortunate over the last ten years to have had very talented, creative, and incredible bakers at the Ivy. They brought their own secret touches, sometimes their own utensils, and always their readiness to try another new recipe.

CARAMEL APPLE TART

CRUST

1 ½ cups flour

1 ½ tbsp. sugar

⅓ cup grated Parmesan cheese

¼ tsp. cayenne pepper

¼ tsp. salt

1 stick cold butter

3 tbsp. ice water

3 tbsp. breadcrumbs

FILLING

5 Granny Smith apples, peeled and sliced

1 cup sugar

3 tbsp. flour

2 tsp. cinnamon

TOPPING

¾ cup sugar

½ cup flour

¼ cup cold butter

1 tsp. vanilla extract

For the crust, mix the flour, sugar, cheese, cayenne pepper, and salt together in an electric mixer. Cut in butter until mixture is coarse crumbs and then add cold water. Do not overmix. Mixture will hold together when pressed between your fingers.

Pour into a well-greased 9-inch springform pan. Press mixture into bottom and up the sides of the pan. Sprinkle breadcrumbs over the crust.

For the filling, gently combine all the ingredients together and then pour into crust.

For the topping, combine all the ingredients together and then sprinkle over the apple filling. Bake at 350 degrees for 60–70 minutes until golden brown on top. Drizzle with warm butterscotch caramel sauce (we use Mrs. Richardson's). Makes 8 to 10 servings.

FRESH APPLE CAKE

Combine oil and sugar together in a bowl; beat in eggs. Sift all dry ingredients together and then add to egg mixture. Fold in vanilla and apples. Pour into a greased 9 x 13-inch pan. Bake at 325 degrees for I hour; set aside to cool.

For the frosting, combine cream cheese and butter in a large bowl using mixer. Gradually add the powdered sugar; beat until smooth and then add vanilla. Frost the cooled cake and then sprinkle pecans over top. Makes 12 to 15 servings.

1 cup canola oil
2 cups sugar
3 eggs
2 ½ cups flour
2 tsp. baking powder
1 tsp. baking soda
1 tsp. salt
2 tsp. ground cinnamon
1 tsp. ground nutmeg
1 tsp. vanilla extract
4 cups peeled and chopped Granny Smith apples

FROSTING
1 (8-oz.) pkg. cream cheese, room temperature
1 stick butter, softened
4 ⅓ cups (about 1 lb.) powdered sugar
2 tsp. vanilla extract
1 cup toasted pecans

FRESH STRAWBERRY CAKE

1 white cake mix
3 tbsp. flour
1 (3-oz.) box
   strawberry gelatin
4 eggs
½ cup water
1 cup vegetable oil
1 cup sliced strawberries

FROSTING
4 ⅓ cups (about 1 lb.)
   powdered sugar
1 stick cold butter
½ cup sliced strawberries

Beat all of the cake ingredients, except strawberry slices, together in an electric mixer for 4 minutes. Stir in strawberries. Grease and paper two 9-inch round cake pans. Divide batter and pour into each pan. Bake at 350 degrees for 35 minutes.

In the meantime, make the frosting. Combine the sugar and butter together and beat for 3 minutes. Add strawberries on low speed, and beat until thoroughly mixed. Do not overbeat. The frosting is more like a ganache. Frost middle and top of cake, but not sides. Drizzle with chocolate or garnish with fresh strawberries on top. Makes 12 servings.

MANDARIN ORANGE CAKE

Mix all the cake ingredients together in an electric mixer and beat for 2 minutes on high speed. Pour batter into a greased 9 x 13-inch pan or two 9-inch-round cake pans that have been greased and lined with parchment paper. Bake at 350 degrees for 25 to 30 minutes; set aside to cool completely.

For the frosting, mix the pudding and crushed pineapple together in an electric mixer and beat for 2 minutes on medium-high speed. Fold whipped topping into mixture, stirring very carefully. Spread over cooled cake, or frost middle and top of layers. Garnish with mandarin orange segments. Makes 12 to 15 servings.

1 yellow cake mix
⅔ cup vegetable oil
½ cup sugar
4 eggs, lightly beaten
1 (9-oz.) can mandarin oranges, with juice

FROSTING

1 small box instant vanilla pudding
1 cup crushed pineapple, with juice
1 (12-oz.) container frozen whipped topping, thawed

RED VELVET CAKE

½ cup shortening
1 ½ cups sugar
2 eggs
¼ cup red food coloring
2 tsp. cocoa, well rounded
1 tsp. salt
2 ¼ cups flour
1 cup buttermilk
1 tsp. vanilla
1 tsp. vinegar
1 tsp. baking soda

FROSTING
¼ cup flour
¾ cup milk
1 ½ sticks butter, softened
¾ cup sugar
2 tbsp. powdered sugar
½ tsp. vanilla

Cream shortening and sugar together until light and fluffy. Add eggs, one at a time, and beat well. Make a paste of food coloring and cocoa and then add to creamed mixture. Mix salt and flour together. Add flour mixture to the creamed mixture alternately with the buttermilk; add vanilla. Mix vinegar and baking soda together—it will foam. Blend and fold vinegar mixture with batter, but do not beat! Pour batter in two 9-inch round cake pans that have been greased and floured or lined with parchment paper. Bake at 350 degrees for 30 minutes; set aside to cool.

For the frosting, cook the flour and milk together in a saucepan over medium heat until thick; let cool. In a mixing bowl, cream remaining ingredients together. Add cooled flour mixture and beat until fluffy. It will take several minutes, but it is worth it! Frost cooled cake and serve. Makes 12 servings.

COCONUT CAKE

Beat the first five cake ingredients together for 4 minutes. Stir in coconut and pecans until well blended. Pour batter in a greased 9 x 13-inch pan. Bake at 350 degrees for 45 to 50 minutes; set aside to cool.

For the frosting, toast the coconut with 2 tbsp. butter in oven, stirring once, at 325 degrees for 10 minutes, or until light brown. Set aside to cool.

Cream remaining butter and cream cheese together until smooth. Gradually add powdered sugar and vanilla; beat until smooth. If frosting is too thick, add a little cream. Stir in 1 3/4 cups toasted coconut and then frost the cake. Garnish with the remaining toasted coconut sprinkled on top of cake. Makes 12 to 15 servings.

1 box yellow cake mix
1 (3.4-oz.) pkg. instant vanilla pudding
1 1/3 cups water
4 eggs
1/4 cup vegetable oil
2 cups shredded coconut
1 cup chopped pecans

FROSTING

2 cups shredded coconut
4 tbsp. butter, divided
1 (8-oz.) pkg. cream cheese, room temperature
3 1/3 cups powdered sugar
1 tsp. vanilla

CARROT-PINEAPPLE-PECAN CAKE

2 cups crushed pineapple,
  with juice
2 cups flour
2 tsp. baking soda
2 cups sugar
2 eggs
2 cups shredded carrots
1 cup chopped pecans
1 tsp. salt

FROSTING
1 8-oz. pkg. cream cheese,
  room temperature
1 stick butter, melted
2 cups powdered sugar
1 tsp. vanilla extract

Mix all the cake ingredients together in an electric mixer until combined. Pour batter into a greased 9 x 13-inch glass pan. Bake at 350 degrees for 35 to 45 minutes, or until a toothpick inserted in the center comes out clean.

For the frosting, beat all the ingredients together until smooth. Frost cake while still warm. Makes 12 servings.

PRAIRIE OATMEAL CAKE

Combine the oatmeal, butter, and hot water together and let stand for 20 minutes. Add the remaining cake ingredients and combine thoroughly. Pour batter into a greased 9 x 13-inch pan. Bake at 350 degrees for 35 minutes.

For the topping, heat the first three ingredients together until the butter is melted. Add remaining ingredients and mix well. Spread on hot cake and broil for 1 to 2 minutes. Makes 12 to 15 servings.

1 ½ cups oatmeal
1 ½ sticks butter
1 ¾ cups hot water
3 eggs, beaten
1 ½ cups brown sugar
1 ½ cups white sugar
2 cups flour
¾ tsp. salt
¾ tsp. nutmeg
1 ½ tsp. cinnamon
1 ½ tsp. baking soda

TOPPING
¾ cup evaporated milk
6 tbsp. butter
1 ½ cups sugar
1 ½ cups chopped pecans
1 ½ cups shredded
coconut
3 tsp. vanilla extract

CRANBERRY CAKE

4 ½ tbsp. butter
1 ½ cups sugar
2 eggs
3 cups flour
3 tsp. baking powder
1 ½ tsp. nutmeg
1 ½ cups milk
1 (12-oz.) pkg. cranberries
  (no need to defrost
  if frozen)
3 tbsp. grated orange or
  lemon peel

CREAM SAUCE

1 ⅓ cups sugar
1 cup heavy cream
⅔ cup butter

In a mixing bowl, cream butter and sugar together until light; beat in eggs. Combine the flour, baking powder, and nutmeg. Add to the creamed mixture alternately with the milk. Stir in the cranberries and orange or lemon peel. Pour batter into a 9 x 13-inch greased glass pan. Bake at 325 degrees for 45 minutes, or until toothpick inserted in the center comes out clean.

While cake is baking, mix all the Cream Sauce ingredients in a saucepan over medium-low heat, stirring until heated thoroughly. While cake is still hot, poke holes all over the top using a straw. Slowly pour the cream sauce over the cake, taking time to allow the sauce to be absorbed. Sweet and tart! Makes 12 to 15 servings.

MRS. NICHOLSON'S PECAN PIE

3 eggs, lightly beaten
½ cup sugar
1 cup light Karo syrup
1 tsp. vanilla
Pinch of salt
1 cup pecans
1 9-in. pie shell, unbaked

Mix eggs, sugar, syrup, vanilla, and salt together until combined. Add pecans and then pour into unbaked pie shell. Bake at 350 degrees for 1 hour. Cool before serving. Makes 6 to 8 servings.

GRANNY HIGBY'S PINEAPPLE PIE

Drain pineapple but reserve $1/2$ cup of the juice, or add enough water to the juice to make $1/2$ cup if necessary.

Pour the juice back into the pineapple and then add the butter. Mix flour and sugar together; add pineapple mixture. Pour into I pie shell and then sprinkle with nutmeg. Roll out remaining pie shell and slice into I-inch strips. Lattice strips over top of pie. Bake at 350 degrees until golden brown, approximately 30 to 40 minutes. Makes 6 to 8 servings.

1 (16-oz.) can crushed
  pineapple
1 stick butter, melted
3 tbsp. flour
1 cup sugar
2 unbaked 9-in. pie shells
Nutmeg

APPLE PIE

Toss apples with sugar, flour, and cinnamon and pour into bottom crust. Dot apple mixture with butter. Gently place top crust over pie. Trim top crust, folding under bottom crust and crimp; cut steam vents. Cover edge of pie with foil to prevent burning. Bake at 375 degrees for 25 minutes. Remove foil and continue to bake 25 minutes more, or until pie is bubbling in the middle; let cool.

Mix all the glaze ingredients together, stirring until smooth. Drizzle over top of the pie and then serve. Makes 8 pieces

5 ½ cups peeled
  and thinly sliced
  Granny Smith apples
1 cup sugar
2 tbsp. flour
1 tsp. cinnamon
2 (9-in.) double crust
  pie shells
1 tbsp. butter

GLAZE
2 cups powdered sugar
2 tbsp. half-and-half
1 tbsp. butter, melted
1 tsp. vanilla extract

FRESH STRAWBERRY PIE

CRUST

½ cup butter, melted

1 tbsp. sugar

1 ½ cups flour

GLAZE AND FILLING

1 cups sugar

3 tbsp. cornstarch

2 tbsp. corn syrup

1 ½ cups water

1 (3-oz.) box
   strawberry gelatin

4 cups sliced strawberries

Combine all the crust ingredients together and then press into a 9-inch pie pan. Bake at 425 degrees for 10 to 15 minutes, or until lightly browned; cool.

Stir the first four glaze ingredients together in a saucepan. Cook over medium-high heat, stirring constantly, until thick and bubbly. Stir in strawberry gelatin and then set aside to cool.

Place sliced strawberries in cooled pie shell. Carefully spoon glaze over strawberries and refrigerate until firm. Serve with whipped cream.

Variation: When peaches are ripe, make the above recipe substituting peaches and apricot gelatin for strawberries and strawberry gelatin. Makes 6 to 8 servings.

JEAN'S CHOCOLATE CHESS PIE

¾ stick butter, melted

1 ½ cups sugar

3 tbsp. cocoa

1 tsp. vanilla extract

1 (5.33 oz.) can
   evaporated milk

2 eggs

1 9-in. pie crust, unbaked

In an electric mixer, beat together all ingredients, except pie crust, until combined. Pour into unbaked pie crust and then bake at 350 degrees for 40 to 50 minutes. Serve warm with whipped cream (not non-dairy whipped topping). Divine! Makes 6 to 8 servings.

APPLE-BLACKBERRY PIE

Place first four ingredients in a food processor and pulse just until coarse crumbs; set aside.

Mix apples, blackberries, sugar, flour, and lemon juice together and then pour into pie shell. Sprinkle crumb topping over top.

Bake at 375 degrees for 25 minutes with foil covering edges of pie to prevent burning. Remove foil and bake another 30 minutes, or until bubbling in the middle; let cool. Makes 8 servings.

¾ cup flour
½ cup brown sugar
½ cup toasted pecans
6 tbsp. butter, chilled
5 Granny Smith apples, sliced
1 cup blackberries
1 cup sugar
4 tbsp. flour
2 tbsp. lemon juice
1 9-in. unbaked pie shell

DEB'S RHUBARB CUSTARD PIE

Preheat oven to 450 degrees. Place rhubarb in unbaked pie shell. Mix flour, eggs, and sugar together until well blended; pour over rhubarb. Sprinkle with nutmeg and drizzle butter over top.

Bake for 10 minutes, and then reduce heat to 350 degrees and bake for 50 minutes. Allow time to set up before serving. Makes 8 servings.

3 cups fresh or frozen rhubarb, cut in 1-in. pieces
1 unbaked 9-in. pie shell
3 tbsp. flour
3 eggs, beaten
1 ¾ cups sugar
½ tsp. nutmeg
1 tbsp. butter, melted

RHUBARB SWIRL PIE

3 cups frozen rhubarb
¾ cup sugar
1 (3-oz.) box
   strawberry gelatin
1 cup heavy
   whipping cream
2 tbsp. sugar
1 tsp. vanilla extract
1 ½ cups milk
1 (3-oz.) box instant
   vanilla pudding
1 baked 10-in. pie crust

In a large saucepan, mix the rhubarb and sugar together, then let stand for 30 minutes. Cook over medium-high heat until tender and thickened. Stir in gelatin until dissolved. Let cool to room temperature.

In a bowl, whip the cream until fluffy. Gradually add the sugar and vanilla; set aside.

In another bowl, whip the milk and instant pudding together on low speed for 2 minutes. Stir the pudding mixture and the whipped cream mixture together.

To assemble, place scant 2 cups pudding mixture into baked shell and then 1 scant cup rhubarb. Swirl slightly with knife tip. Add remaining pudding and rhubarb and swirl again.

Refrigerate several hours or overnight to set. Scrumptious! Makes 8 servings.

PEGGY'S PIE CRUST

1 ½ cups flour
½ tsp. salt
½ cup lard
4 to 5 tbsp. ice water

Mix together the flour and salt. Cut in lard. Stir in ice water just until dough sticks together. Chill before rolling out. Makes 1 10-inch pie shell.

COCONUT CREAM PIE

Mix 1 cup sugar, salt, cornstarch, and milk together over medium heat in a saucepan; let boil 1 minute and then remove from heat. Add egg yolks and bring back to a boil; let boil 1 minute. Add 1 teaspoon vanilla extract, butter, and 1 cup coconut. Take off heat and stir until thoroughly combined.

In a bowl, beat egg whites with cream of tartar until soft peaks form. Add remaining sugar, a tablespoon at a time, until peaks become stiff and glossy. Top pie with meringue and then sprinkle remaining coconut on top. Bake at 325 degrees for 15 to 18 minutes, or until meringue is light brown. Let cool before serving. Makes 8 servings.

1 ¾ cups sugar, divided
½ tsp. salt
½ cup cornstarch
3 ¾ cups milk
6 eggs, separated
2 tsp. vanilla extract, divided
2 tbsp. butter
1 ¼ cups shredded coconut, divided
½ tsp. cream of tartar
1 baked 10-in. pie shell

PUMPKIN PIE

In a bowl, combine eggs, pumpkin, sugar, and spices. Add milk and mix thoroughly. Pour into unbaked pie crust and bake at 450 degrees for 15 minutes. Reduce heat to 350 degrees and continue baking for 45 minutes more. Pie is done when a knife inserted in the center comes out clean. Makes 8 servings.

3 eggs, beaten
2 ½ cups pumpkin
1 cup sugar
¾ tsp. salt
1 ½ tsp. cinnamon
¾ tsp. ginger
½ tsp. ground cloves
½ tsp. nutmeg
1 (12 oz.) can evaporated milk
1 unbaked 10-in. pie crust

breads & breakfast pastries

The new millennium! We had a contest, chose a new dessert (the Millennium Bar, of course) and settled into the new year with enthusiasm and new recipes to be sampled. Little did we know that life for the Ivy Bake Shoppe was going to change radically over the next several years.

The previous year, we had been honored by the Iowa Small Business Development Center and were awarded the Deb Dalziel Woman Entrepreneur Achievement Award. This award brought us statewide publicity.

Publicity is a powerful tool. Once established, it takes on a life of its own, and such was the case for the Ivy. We were featured in the April/May 2000 issue of *The Iowa Commerce Magazine* in an article focusing on entrepreneurs. Suddenly, we were being discovered outside of southeastern Iowa.

Then *Time* magazine writer Steve Lopez fell in love with Fort Madison and the Ivy's Blackberry Scones while doing an article on Mississippi River towns. Talk about dumb luck! We had a national journalist writing an article for a huge publication about Fort Madison's viable downtown, and in the article he describes the scones from the Ivy. The article appeared in the July 2000 *Time* issue and revitalized the spirit of our community, created positive synergy, and took the Ivy nationwide.

Remarkably, more and more people opened the door to the Ivy, magazine under their arm, wanting to try the Blackberry Scones and other delectable offerings. The guestbook at our front door is a journal of hundreds of people from all over the country sharing a meal and some great conversation in this small Iowa town.

BLACKBERRY SCONES

4 cups flour
4 tsp. baking powder
1 tsp. baking soda
1 tsp. cream of tartar
½ tsp. salt
1 ½ sticks butter, cold
¾ cup buttermilk
¾ cup heavy cream
1 egg
2 ½ cups blackberries
   (or other fruit), divided

GLAZE
1 cup powdered sugar
¼ cup milk

Mix all the dry ingredients in a stand mixer. Add cold butter that has been cut in 6 to 8 slices. Mix on low until pea size with some small butter chunks still evident.

Mix buttermilk, cream, and egg together until combined. Slowly pour into butter mixture with mixer running on low. Mix briefly until combined, taking care to not overbeat. Pour out onto floured board and knead dough four or five times; cut in half. Roll out half of the dough to about 1/2 inch thick. Pour 1 1/4 cups blackberries over dough and fold over. Roll out once again to 3/4 inch thick; cut into 6 wedges. Repeat with second half of dough. Place scones on greased baking sheets. Brush with some extra cream and sprinkle with sugar. Bake at 425 degrees for 13 minutes. Drizzle glaze over top and then sprinkle with powdered sugar. Makes 12 scones.

Note: They freeze great precooked. However, let them sit out at room temperature for 45 to 60 minutes before baking.

LEMON CRANBERRY SCONES

Stir the flour, baking powder, lemon peel, salt, and sugar in a mixing bowl. Add the butter and beat on low for a couple of minutes, or until coarse meal forms. Mix in nuts and cranberries. Add the cream, egg, and lemon juice. Mix on low until all dough is moist clumps. Turn out on a lightly floured board and gather dough into a ball. Divide in half, and press or roll each half into a 5- or 6-inch circle; cut each into 6 wedges. Place on a greased baking sheet. Bake at 400 degrees for 12 to 14 minutes, or until golden. Mix the glaze ingredients together and then brush warm scones with glaze. Makes 12 servings.

3 cups flour
1 ½ tbsp. baking powder
1 tbsp. lemon peel
1 tsp. salt
1 cup sugar
1 ½ sticks cold butter, sliced in pieces
½ cup chopped pecans
1 cup dried cranberries
¾ cup cream
1 egg
1 tbsp. lemon juice

GLAZE
2 tbsp. sugar
1 tbsp. lemon juice

BETTE LEE'S CINNAMON LOGS

Mix cinnamon and 1 cup sugar together and set aside.

Beat egg yolks, ½ cup sugar, and cream cheese together until smooth. Spread mixture on bread slices and roll up. Dip rolls in melted butter and then in cinnamon and sugar mixture.

Place on a baking sheet and freeze. When ready to use, take directly out of freezer and bake at 400 degrees for 10 to 15 minutes, or until lightly brown. So good! Makes 20 to 24 servings.

1 tbsp. cinnamon
1 cup sugar
2 egg yolks
½ cup sugar
2 (8-oz.) pkg. cream cheese
1 ½ loaves sandwich bread with crusts removed
1 ½ sticks butter, melted

CINNAMON ROLLS

1 ¼ cups milk

¼ cup shortening

¼ cup sugar

1 pkg. or 1 tbsp. yeast

1 tsp. coarse salt

3 ¼ cups high gluten
   or bread flour, divided

1 egg

¾ stick butter, divided

½ cup sugar

1 tbsp. cinnamon

2 cups powdered sugar

Cream

Heat milk, shortening, and sugar in a saucepan over medium heat to 120 degrees, stirring to melt sugar and shortening. In a large mixing bowl, combine the yeast, salt, and 1 ½ cups flour. When milk mixture reaches 120 degrees, pour into flour mixture and mix on low for 1 minute. Add egg, and then beat for 2 or 3 minutes on medium speed. On low speed, begin adding remaining flour, ½ cup at a time. When dough pulls away from side of bowl, is very soft, and does not stick to your finger, it has enough flour. You may not need all of the flour. Turn out onto a floured board. Knead just until thoroughly combined. Place in a greased bowl, and turn once, so top is greased. Cover and let rise in a warm place for 1 hour. Punch down, cover, and let rest for 10 minutes.

Roll out dough into a rectangle about 10 x 15 inches. Soften 4 tablespoons butter and spread to cover the dough. Sprinkle with sugar and cinnamon. Roll up tightly like a jellyroll along the 15-inch side and turn in ends and seal edges. Cut into 10 to 12 rolls, placing cut side down on a greased baking sheet.

Melt rest of butter and brush tops of rolls; let rise 45 minutes. Bake at 375 degrees for 13 minutes, or until golden brown. Combine powdered sugar and cream to spreading consistency and then frost warm rolls. Makes 10 to 12 rolls.

CARAMEL ROLLS

In a saucepan over medium heat, melt the butter and then add the sugar, corn syrup, and cream, stirring constantly. Pour into a jellyroll pan and top with pecans.

Follow Cinnamon Roll recipe on page 98 to make the dough. After spreading dough with 4 tablespoons butter, sprinkle brown sugar and cinnamon over top; roll up. Place rolls cut side down on top of pecan mixture. Bake at 375 degrees for 13 to 15 minutes. Sauce may boil over, so place the jellyroll pan on a larger baking sheet when placing in oven.

Cover rolls with another pan and let cool for 2 minutes. Carefully invert rolls onto top pan. Makes 10 to 12 rolls.

1 ¼ sticks butter
1 ½ cups packed
   brown sugar
5 tbsp. corn syrup
4 tbsp. heavy cream
1 ½ cups chopped pecans
¾ stick butter, divided
1 cup brown sugar
1 tbsp. cinnamon

ORANGE ROLLS

2 cups milk

½ cup sugar

½ cup shortening

1 tbsp. (1 pkg.) yeast

2 tsp. salt

7 cups flour, divided

2 eggs, beaten

1 tsp. lemon extract

FILLING

2 tbsp. grated orange peel

1 cup sugar

½ cup butter, softened

½ cup orange juice

GLAZE

4 cups powdered sugar

Orange juice

Heat milk, sugar, and shortening in a saucepan to 115 degrees. In mixing bowl with paddle attachment, place yeast, salt, and 3 cups flour. Pour in heated liquid and beat for 2 minutes on medium speed.

Add beaten eggs and lemon extract. Slowly add rest of flour and beat until dough pulls away from side of bowl. Pour into a greased bowl, and turn one time. Cover with damp towel, and let rise about 1 hour. Pour out of bowl onto floured table. Cover and let rest 10 minutes. Roll out dough on a floured board into a large rectangle.

For the filling, mix all ingredients together thoroughly. Spread dough with filling and carefully roll up, tucking in the ends. Slice and place on a greased baking sheet. Cover with plastic wrap and let rise in a warm place for 45 minutes. Bake at 350 degrees until lightly brown, about 12 to 15 minutes. Make glaze while rolls are baking. Combine powdered sugar with enough orange juice to make a glaze consistency. Glaze rolls while still warm. Makes approximately 20 small rolls.

RHUBARB BRUNCH CAKE

Cream butter and sugar in a mixing bowl until light and fluffy. Add next six ingredients and then stir in rhubarb. Pour into a greased 9 x 13-inch glass dish. Sprinkle with brown sugar and pecans. Bake at 350 degrees for 1 hour.

Combine all the sauce ingredients together in a saucepan and cook over low heat until sugar dissolves. Let cake cool for about 10 minutes and then pour sauce over top of cake. Serve warm. Makes 12 to 15 servings.

1 stick butter
1 ½ cups sugar
1 egg
1 tsp. baking soda
½ tsp. salt
3 cups flour
1 cup buttermilk
1 tsp. vanilla extract
3 cups sliced rhubarb
1 cup brown sugar
1 cup chopped pecans

SAUCE
1 stick butter
½ cup evaporated milk
1 cup sugar
1 tsp. vanilla extract

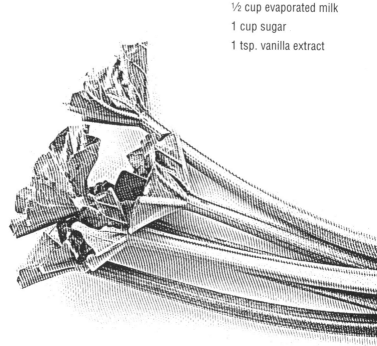

KATHY'S PISTACHIO NUT BREAD

1 yellow cake mix
½ cup vegetable oil
4 large eggs
1 cup warm water
2 small boxes instant
   pistachio pudding

Combine all ingredients together and beat with an electric mixer for 4 minutes on medium-high speed. Pour batter into greased loaf pans. Bake at 325 degrees for 25 to 30 minutes, or until toothpick inserted in center comes out clean. Cool in pan for 10 minutes and then remove. When loaves are completely cool, dust with powdered sugar. This recipe makes 2 to 3 medium-size loaves, or 4 to 5 mini loaf pans (bake 18 to 22 minutes). If making cupcakes, fill very full and bake 18 to 22 minutes.

PECAN SOUR CREAM MUFFINS

1 white cake mix
¾ cup vegetable oil
½ cup sugar
1 cup sour cream
4 eggs

CINNAMON SUGAR
2 tsp. cinnamon
3 tbsp. sugar

GLAZE
½ cup powdered sugar
2 tbsp. milk
½ tsp. vanilla
½ cup chopped pecans
   (optional)

Beat together the first four ingredients in an electric mixer on high for 3 minutes. Add eggs, one at a time, beating after each addition. Line muffin pans with liners. Fill muffin cups 3/4 full. Sprinkle with cinnamon sugar. Top with chopped pecans if desired. Bake at 325 degrees for 20 to 25 minutes. Mix all the glaze ingredients together and drizzle over muffins. Makes 24 muffins.

CARROT-CRAISIN-BRAN MUFFINS

Pour bran into a large bowl. Mix dry ingredients together and then add to bran. Combine eggs, buttermilk, and oil and then add to flour mixture; fold in carrots, mixing thoroughly. Line a muffin pan with liners. Fill muffin cups 3/4 full. Bake at 350 degrees for 25 minutes. Makes 2 1/2 dozen muffins.

Note: Batter will keep in the refrigerator for 6 weeks, and baked muffins freeze great.

1 (15- to 17-oz.) box oat bran cereal
2 cups sugar
5 cups flour
5 tsp. baking soda
2 tsp. salt
2 cups Craisins
4 eggs, slightly beaten
1 qt. buttermilk
1 cup salad oil
3 cups shredded carrots

THE OTHER SUSAN'S ORANGE NECTAR CAKE

Place first four ingredients in a mixing bowl with 3 egg yolks; beat 4 minutes. In a separate bowl, beat 3 egg whites until stiff. Fold into mixture lightly. Grease and flour a loaf or Bundt pan and then pour in batter. Bake at 350 degrees for 40 minutes, or until golden on top. Stir glaze ingredients together until smooth. Pour or brush over cake while cake is still warm. Makes 8 to 12 servings.

Note: This recipe also makes 2 dozen muffins. Bake at 350 degrees for about 20 to 25 minutes.

1 lemon cake mix
1 cup orange juice
½ cup sugar
⅔ cup vegetable oil
3 eggs, separated

GLAZE
1 cup powdered sugar
¼ cup orange juice

ELIZABETH'S POPPY SEED BREAD

3 cups flour
1 ½ tsp. salt
1 ½ tsp. baking powder
2 ¼ cups sugar
3 eggs
1 ½ cups milk
1 cup plus 2 tbsp. oil
4 tbsp. poppy seeds
1 ½ tsp. vanilla extract
1 ½ tsp. almond extract

GLAZE
¾ cup powdered sugar
¼ tsp. almond extract
½ tsp. vanilla extract
¼ cup orange juice

Put all ingredients together in a mixing bowl and beat for 2 minutes. Pour batter into two floured and greased 7 ½ x 3 ¾ x 2 ¼-inch bread pans. Bake at 350 degrees for 55 minutes. Let cool on a rack 5 minutes.

For the glaze, mix all ingredients together. Pour over bread. Let cool in pans 10 minutes. Remove from pans and finish cooling on rack.

Makes 6 mini loaf pans (bake 20 to 25 minutes) or 11 dozen mini muffins (bake 15 minutes).

LEMON POPPY SEED CAKE

In a mixing bowl, combine oil, buttermilk, ¼ cup lemon juice, pudding, cake mix, and three-fourths of the lemon zest. Mix with an electric mixer until blended; add eggs and beat well, scraping down sides of bowl occasionally. Stir in poppy seeds. Pour into a well-greased and floured Bundt pan; batter will be very thick. Bake at 350 degrees for approximately 40 to 50 minutes, or until a toothpick inserted in the center comes out clean. Let cool 20 minutes before turning out onto a cooling rack.

In a bowl, mix 2 tablespoons lemon juice with the remaining zest. Add powdered sugar. Stir in half-and-half until the consistency of glaze. Pour over warm cake. Makes 8 to 12 servings.

Note: This recipe will make 6 mini Bundt cakes. Bake at 350 degrees for 30 to 40 minutes.

½ cup vegetable oil
½ cup buttermilk
Juice of 2 lemons, divided
1 small box vanilla instant pudding
1 white cake mix
Zest of 2 lemons, divided
4 eggs
⅓ cup poppy seeds
2 cups powdered sugar
Half-and-half

JEANNE'S DUTCH ALMOND BARS

DOUGH

3 cups flour

¼ cup sugar

½ tsp. salt

1 ½ sticks cold butter,
 cut up

1 ½ tbsp. ice water

FILLING

1 (8-oz.) can pure
 almond paste

⅓ cup sugar

1 egg

1 tbsp. pure almond extract

1 egg

1 tbsp. cream

Sugar

For the dough, sift the dry ingredients into a stand mixer. Add butter and process until small pea-size granules form. Slowly add the ice water until dough holds together. Divide into 3 equal-size balls. Wrap and refrigerate for 30 minutes.

For the filling, beat all four ingredients with mixer until smooth. Refrigerate in the bowl.

When ready, lightly flour work surface and roll out dough. Roll each ball into a 12-inch-long rectangle strip and spread each with one-third of the filling down the center and up close to each end. Fold up the sides to meet, pinch closed, and then close ends. Smooth out the top using the egg mixed with cream.

Transfer three logs to a greased jellyroll pan; chill 20 minutes. Preheat oven to 375 degrees. Prick rolls with fork just on the surface. Sprinkle with sugar or raw cane sugar. Turn oven down to 350 degrees and bake for 30 minutes. Cool in pan and then cut each log into 4 bars.

CHOCOLATE BISCOTTI

Mix all the dry ingredients together. Make a well in center and add remaining ingredients, mixing thoroughly. Knead dough to incorporate ingredients; then form 3 loaves and place on an ungreased baking sheet. Bake at 325 degrees for 30 minutes; let cool. Slice in thin pieces and place on baking sheet. Return to oven at 300 degrees and bake for 20 minutes more. We garnish with melted white chocolate drizzled over top. Makes 30 pieces.

2 ⅔ cups flour
1 cup cocoa
1 ½ tsp. baking soda
¼ tsp. salt
2 cups sugar
1 ¾ cups chopped pecans, toasted
⅔ cup miniature chocolate chips
2 tbsp. coffee
5 eggs
1 ½ tsp. vanilla extract

SARA DICHIARA'S MANDELBROT

Preheat oven to 350 degrees. Pour dry ingredients into a mixing bowl and stir well. Make a well in the center. Add remaining ingredients and mix well. Knead until smooth enough that it doesn't stick to your fingers. Form 3 loaves, each 6 to 7 inches long and 1 ½ inches thick. Place on an ungreased baking sheet about 2 inches apart. Bake 30 to 45 minutes, or until light brown; allow to cool. Slice thinly; place on baking sheet and toast 15 minutes, or until brown. Will keep for weeks in an air-tight container. Makes about 48 slices.

1 ¼ cups sugar
3 cups flour
1 tsp. baking powder
¾ cup vegetable oil
3 eggs
1 ½ tsp. vanilla extract
¾ cup chopped pecans

PERFECT SISTER SUSAN'S SWEDISH TEA CAKES

1 package dry yeast
¼ cup warm water
2 ¼ cups flour
2 tbsp. sugar
1 tsp. salt
½ cup butter
¼ cup evaporated milk
1 egg
¼ cup Craisins

FILLING

¼ cup butter, softened
½ cup light brown sugar

ICING

2 tbsp. butter
1 cup sifted powdered
  sugar
1 tsp. pure vanilla extract
2 tbsp. evaporated milk
½ cup toasted pecans for
  garnish (optional)

Soften yeast in warm water. Mix flour, sugar, and salt in a mixing bowl with paddle attachment. Mix in butter until particles are fine. Add evaporated milk, egg, Craisins, and yeast to flour and butter mixture. Mix well on low speed. Cover and chill in refrigerator at least 3 hours or overnight.

Make the filling when ready to roll out the dough. Cream butter and brown sugar until thoroughly combined. Divide dough into 3 equal parts. On a floured surface, roll one part to a 6 x 12-inch rectangle. Spread with one-third of the filling. Roll up, starting with the longer side. Seal by pinching dough together. Form roll into a crescent shape and place on a cookie sheet lined with foil or parchment paper. Make ¹/₂-inch cuts along the outside edge of crescent, about 1 inch apart. Repeat with remaining portions of dough. Let crescents rise in a warm place until light, about 45 minutes. Bake at 350 degrees for 20 to 25 minutes, or until golden brown. Frost with icing while hot.

To make icing, brown butter in a small iron skillet. Add powdered sugar and vanilla. Stir in evaporated milk until it is of spreading consistency, adding more evaporated milk if necessary. Spread icing on tea cakes while still warm. Sprinkle with pecans if desired. Serve slightly warm, cut in small pieces. Freezes great! Makes 8 to 10 servings.

DODIE'S DILLY CHEESE BREAD

Soften yeast in warm water. In a saucepan, heat cottage cheese to lukewarm. Stir in shortening, sugar, onion, dill, salt, baking soda, and yeast mixture. Beat in egg. Add flour a little bit at a time, stirring to make a soft dough. Knead on a lightly floured surface until smooth and elastic, about 5 minutes. Place in a greased bowl, turning once. Cover and let rise in a warm place for 1 hour. Punch down, cover and let rest 10 minutes. Shape into a loaf and place in a greased loaf pan. Cover and let rise again for 30 to 45 minutes. Bake at 350 degrees for 40 minutes. Remove from pan and brush with melted butter. Sprinkle with additional dill if desired. Makes 6 to 8 servings.

1 pkg. dry yeast
¼ cup warm water
1 cup cottage cheese
¼ cup shortening
2 tbsp. sugar
1 tbsp. minced onion
2 tsp. dill weed
1 tsp. salt
¼ tsp. baking soda
1 egg, well beaten
2 ¼ to 2 ½ cups flour
Melted butter

FOCACCIA BREAD

1 ¼ cups mashed potatoes
½ cup milk
2 ½ cups high gluten or
  bread flour, divided
1 tbsp. coarse salt
½ cup basil olive oil
1 ½ tbsp. yeast
½ cup chopped red onion
1 cup feta cheese,
  crumbled and divided
Olive oil for drizzling

Grease a 12 x 14-inch sheet pan.

In a saucepan, gently warm potatoes and milk to 120 degrees. Place in a stand mixer with a dough hook. Add 1 cup flour, salt, olive oil, and yeast. Mix on low for 30 seconds, until well blended. Add remaining flour, onion, and half of the feta cheese. Mix on low speed for 5 to 6 minutes, or knead by hand for 8 to 10 minutes. Oil top of dough, and turn once. Cover and let rise until double in size, about 45 to 60 minutes. (Or refrigerate overnight instead of letting it rise and then bring to room temperature before continuing).

Roll out dough on a floured surface and place in greased pan, stretching dough to fit pan. Pierce dough over entire surface. Drizzle with olive oil and sprinkle with remaining feta cheese. Let rise until double, about 30 minutes.

Bake at 400 degrees for 20 minutes, or until golden brown. Makes 8 to 12 servings.

REUBEN BREAD

Mix yeast in warm water with sugar to dissolve. In the bowl of a stand mixer, add 2 cups flour, salt, and butter. Add yeast mixture and beat on high speed for 30 seconds. Slowly add remaining flour to make a soft dough. Cover with a damp cloth and let rest for 10 minutes. Roll out into a 9 x 13-inch rectangle, with the short end facing you. Spread dressing down middle third of dough. Layer with corned beef, sauerkraut, and Swiss cheese. Make slits along each side of dough to braid over filling. Starting at the top, alternate closing the bread with each slit. Transfer to a greased baking sheet. Cover and let rest for 30 to 45 minutes. Brush dough with melted butter and then place in oven. Bake at 400 degrees for 20 to 25 minutes, or until golden brown. Makes 4 to 8 servings.

1 pkg. yeast
1 cup warm water
  (115 degrees)
2 tsp. sugar
3 cups high gluten
  or bread flour, divided
1 tsp. kosher coarse salt
2 tbsp. butter, softened
½ cup Thousand Island
  dressing
½ lb. corned beef, cut in
  thin strips
2 cups sauerkraut
1 cup grated Swiss cheese
Melted butter

NOTES

———— side dishes ————

I n the fall of 2000, Greg Shottenkirk, a local resident and
owner of several car dealerships, approached Sue and me
about opening a second store inside a new dealership he
was building in Burlington. Burlington is a community of
about 30,000 residents located about 20 miles north of Fort
Madison. We were flabbergasted, astounded, and speechless.
He showed us the blueprints where the Ivy had been penciled
in, and asked that we seriously consider the opportunity.

Because I am not a "finance person" by nature, I had taken
several entrepreneurial classes offered by the Small Business
Development Center. The classes offered networking with
other entrepreneurs, helped clarify business plans, taught
how to read the numbers, assisted in establishing a marketing
plan, stressed the importance of planning an exit strategy, and
overall taught a great grasp of "running the business, instead
of the business running you!" More importantly for us at that
moment, they offered us skilled personnel who could project
the numbers and help us determine if this was a viable move.
Three days later we told Greg, "YES!"

We immediately solicited Tom Wolf's talent in designing the
new space, using renovated and refurbished materials to assure
the feel and atmosphere of our original Ivy in Fort Madison.
This time around, we built a totally commercial kitchen with
professional equipment. Adding a second store forced us
to be better organized. We put all of our recipes on the computer,
let go, and let our capable staff assume more responsibility,
and then we worked smarter not harder.

The store opened in July 2002, about nine months behind schedule. That certainly worked to our advantage. In the midst of designing and building a new store, we began to notice an influx of missionaries from Nauvoo, Illinois. The Church of Jesus Christ of Latter-day Saints was rebuilding its temple with a projected opening date of June 2002. It was such an incredible time for this area. Starting with the Public Affairs Department and the Interior Designers, we developed wonderful friendships with the missionaries that continue to this day. That summer, 350,000 people visited the temple over a six-week period, and we served 10,000 of them.

Through their grapevine, missionaries from all over the world knew to stop by the Ivy and order Warm Onion Pie, Tortilla Soup, Caramel Rice Krispie Bar, and Strawberry Cake.

The summer of 2002, we opened a new business, greeted and nourished thousands of LDS members, and survived. Challenging and overwhelming at times, the growth added another dimension to the Ivy. It was exhilarating, and our passion continued.

WARM ONION PIE

Melt half the butter and mix with breadcrumbs and salt. Place in a well-greased 8-inch pie pan, and press into bottom and up the sides.

Saute onions in remaining butter slowly, stirring constantly until onions are clear and tender. Remove from heat. Drain onions and place over crust.

Combine flour, cheese, salt, and cayenne pepper. Scald milk, add eggs, and stir. Add milk mixture to cheese mixture. Carefully pour batter over onions. Bake at 350 degrees for approximately 30 minutes, or until golden brown. Makes 6 to 8 servings.

1 stick butter, divided
1 cup breadcrumbs
1 tsp. salt
3 cups diced sweet onions
1 tbsp. flour
2 cups finely grated
   Swiss cheese
1 tsp. salt
¼ tsp. cayenne pepper
1 cup scalded milk
3 eggs, well beaten

RENEE'S TOMATO BASIL PIE

Put ¾ cup mozzarella cheese on the bottom of the pie crust. Cover with tomatoes and then layer basil leaves that have been slivered. Mix garlic, mayonnaise, remaining mozzarella, black pepper, and Parmesan cheese. Carefully spread on top of pie. Bake at 350 degrees for 30 minutes, or until cheese is golden. Unbelievable! Makes 8 servings.

Variation: Substituting spinach leaves for basil creates a different but delicious pie.

1 ½ cups grated mozzarella cheese, divided
1 baked 9-in. pie crust
3 medium-size tomatoes, diced and drained
1 cup fresh basil leaves, loosely measured
1 clove garlic, crushed
¾ cup mayonnaise
¼ tsp. black pepper
¼ cup freshly grated Parmesan cheese

BROCCOLI SALAD

DRESSING
1 cup mayonnaise
½ cup sugar
2 tbsp. red wine vinegar

SALAD
8 cups broccoli, cut up
½ cup raisins or craisins
½ cup crumbled,
  cooked bacon
Red onion rings (optional)
Mandarin oranges
  (optional)

Mix dressing thoroughly. Let dressing blend overnight in the refrigerator.

Mix remaining ingredients together. Pour dressing over mixture and stir until well coated. Serve! Makes 8 to 10 servings.

DEVILED EGGS

6 hard-boiled eggs
⅛ tsp. garlic powder
1 tsp. dry mustard
⅛ tsp. celery salt
½ tsp. coarse pepper
½ cup mayonnaise

Cut eggs in half lengthwise and carefully remove yolk. Put yolk in food processor and then add rest of ingredients except paprika, processing until there are no lumps. Fill each white egg half with filling. Sprinkle lightly with paprika. Serve on a bed of lettuce. Makes 4 to 6 servings.

SIDE DISHES

COTTAGE CHEESE VEGETABLE MEDLEY

Mix all ingredients together until well combined; refrigerate. Actually adaptable to using any finely diced vegetables available. Makes 4 to 6 servings.

3 cups cottage cheese
½ cup shredded carrots
¼ cup shredded radishes
¼ cup finely diced green bell pepper
2 green onions, finely diced
½ cucumber, peeled, pulp removed, and chopped finely
1 tbsp. dill weed
1 tsp. Lawry's seasoned salt

KITTY'S PASTA

Cook and drain pasta following package directions; do not rinse. Let cool and sprinkle liberally with seasoned salt. Put pasta in a bowl and pour mixture of lemon juice and oil over it; chill. Add the remaining ingredients once pasta is chilled. It is better stored in a flat pan so all the vegetables don't sink to the bottom. Makes 6 to 8 servings.

1 (8-oz.) pkg. thin spaghetti or vermicelli
Lawry's seasoned salt, to taste
3 tbsp. lemon juice
3 tbsp. vegetable oil
½ cup chopped green bell peppers
½ cup chopped green onions
½ cup sliced black olives
¼ cup pimientos
1 tbsp. mayonnaise

117

CRUNCHY PEA SALAD

1 (16-oz.) bag frozen peas
1 heaping tbsp. sour cream
1/3 cup ranch salad dressing
1 (8-oz.) can water
  chestnuts, drained
  and cut in half
3 green onions, whites and
  greens, finely chopped
1/2 cup cashew nuts

Rinse peas in a colander to thaw. While draining, stir sour cream and ranch dressing together. Mix peas, water chestnuts, and green onions in a bowl; stir in dressing. If serving immediately, stir in cashews. Otherwise, garnish with cashews when ready to serve. Delightful served on a bed of lettuce. Makes 4 to 6 servings.

TWICE-BAKED POTATOES

4 baking potatoes
1 onion, chopped
1 stick butter
1/8 tsp. cayenne pepper
2 tsp. kosher coarse salt
1/4 tsp. pepper
1 cup grated cheddar cheese
1/3 cup instant potato flakes
1/2 to 3/4 cup heavy cream

Scrub potatoes, dry, and then pierce with a fork. Bake at 425 degrees for 45 minutes to 1 hour, or until tender.

Cook onion in butter on low heat until clear and tender, about 20 to 25 minutes. Halve potatoes lengthwise. Scoop out the pulp, leaving shells intact. Mash the potatoes; add seasonings, onion mixture, cheese, and potato flakes. Beat in enough of the heavy cream for a fluffy consistency; fill shells. May freeze potatoes at this point. Bake at 400 degrees for 20 to 25 minutes, or until golden on tops. To serve from frozen state, let thaw 30 minutes before baking. Makes 6 to 8 servings.

STUFFED PORTABELLO MUSHROOMS

Rub mushroom caps with olive oil and place on a greased baking sheet gill side up. Sprinkle gills with coarse salt and balsamic vinegar. Bake at 400 degrees for 15 minutes.

For the filling, puree the beans and garlic with 4 tablespoons olive oil until very smooth. Transfer to a bowl.

Put all the vegetables on a baking sheet and drizzle with remaining olive oil. Mix well to coat vegetables. Season with thyme, salt, and pepper. Roast at 425 degrees for 15 to 20 minutes, checking and stirring after 10 minutes.

Fill each mushroom cap with white bean puree and then top with roasted vegetables. It is incredibly delicious and healthy. Makes 4 to 6 servings.

6 portabello mushrooms
Olive oil
Coarse salt
Balsamic vinegar

FILLING
1 (15-oz.) can
　cannellini beans
1 clove garlic, chopped
5 tbsp. olive oil, divided
1 medium zucchini, diced
　medium
½ red onion,
　coarsely chopped
¼ head cauliflower,
　cut in florets
1 sweet potato, peeled
　and diced
2 tsp. crushed thyme
Salt and pepper

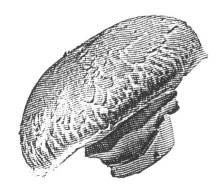

BLACK BEAN AND ROASTED CORN SALAD

1 tbsp. olive oil
1 clove garlic, chopped
4 cups frozen corn
1 can black beans, rinsed
⅓ cup chopped tomatoes
⅓ cup chopped red onion
2 heaping tbsp. salsa
¼ tsp. cayenne pepper
½ tsp. salt
¼ tsp. pepper
Juice of ½ lime
2 tbsp. minced fresh
   cilantro
2 tbsp. chopped fresh
   parsley

Heat olive oil in an iron skillet over medium-high heat. Briefly saute garlic and then add corn. Roast over medium-high heat, stirring constantly. Continue cooking until liquid has been absorbed and some corn kernels are brown; set aside to cool.

Combine remaining ingredients in a large mixing bowl and stir to combine. Add corn once it has cooled; adjust salt and pepper.

This salad has a nice bite, but is not too hot. Makes 8 servings.

APPLE WALDORF SALAD

1 stalk celery, chopped
1 lb. grapes, cut in half
¼ cup apple juice
3 Granny Smith apples,
   cored and chunked
1 cup miniature
   marshmallows
¼ tsp. curry powder
¼ cup mayonnaise
2 cups whipped topping
1 cup toasted walnuts

Mix celery and grapes in apple juice. Add apples (with the peel on) and then add marshmallows.

In a bowl, mix the curry powder with mayonnaise until combined. Softly fold in whipped topping. Stir into fruit and marshmallows; keep refrigerated. When ready to serve, either stir toasted walnuts into salad or use as a garnish. Makes 6 to 8 servings.

JUDY'S CORN BREAD SALAD

Cook corn bread per package directions. Crumble corn bread into a bowl when it comes out of oven.

Add all the vegetables to the corn bread; stir thoroughly. Mix together the ranch dressing, mayonnaise and mustard. Toss lightly and add to the vegetable and corn bread mixture. Serve! Makes 8 servings.

1 pkg. Jiffy corn bread mix
1 small red onion, chopped
½ cup chopped celery
½ cup chopped radishes
½ green or red bell pepper
1 (3-oz.) jar pimientos
3 tomatoes, diced
½ cup ranch salad dressing
½ cup mayonnaise
2 tsp. mustard

MARTHA'S PASTA POTATO SALAD

Cut potatoes into bite-size pieces. Boil for 5 minutes. Check for fork tenderness. If done, drain water. Boil more water and add fusili pasta, cooking per package directions; drain. Cut snow peas in thirds. In a large bowl, combine all the ingredients and mix well.

Stir all the dressing ingredients together and then slowly blend into salad. Makes 10 to 12 servings.

3 lb. red new potatoes
2 cups fusili pasta
½ lb. snow peas, blanched for 1 minute
6 bacon strips, cooked, and crumbled
½ cup chopped fresh mint
½ tsp. salt
½ tsp. coarse pepper

DRESSING
½ to ¾ cup mayonnaise
3 tbsp. sour cream
1 ½ tbsp. cider vinegar

MASCARPONE CREAMED SPINACH

3 tbsp. olive oil
¼ cup chopped shallots
4 cloves garlic, chopped
2 (10-oz.) bags spinach,
   removing stems,
   if necessary
¾ cup mascarpone cheese
¼ cup pine nuts
Salt and pepper

Heat oil in a heavy pot over medium-high heat. Add shallots and garlic and saute until tender, about 3 minutes. Add spinach and toss leaves until they begin to wilt, about 3 minutes. Mix in mascarpone cheese and pine nuts and stir until mascarpone is heated though. Season spinach to taste with salt and pepper. Makes 6 to 8 servings.

GARLIC CHEESE GRITS

4 cups water
2 tsp. salt
1 cup grits, uncooked
1 stick butter
1 roll garlic cheese
½ lb. sharp cheese, grated
2 tbsp. Worcestershire
   sauce
Paprika

Bring the water and salt to a rolling boil and then stir in the grits. Mix thoroughly and reduce heat to low; cover. Stir occasionally to prevent the grits from sticking. Cook about 3 to 4 minutes until water is absorbed. When cooked, add the butter, garlic cheese, sharp cheese, and Worcestershire sauce. Stir until the butter and cheese have melted. Put mixture in a greased 2-quart casserole dish and sprinkle with paprika. Bake at 350 degrees for 15 to 20 minutes. Makes 8 to 10 servings as a side, unless everyone loves grits!

BASIL PESTO

Process almonds and garlic in a food processor. Add spinach, basil, and cheese; pulse. While machine is running, add oil in a thin stream. Stir until combined; adjust seasonings. Package and store in refrigerator or freezer.

We add 1 1/2 cups mayonnaise to 4 ounces Basil Pesto for the Pesto Mayonnaise that we serve on our Veggie Sandwich. We package in 4-ounce containers and freeze for 6 to 8 months. Also great with pasta! Makes about 14 to 16 ounces of pesto.

1/2 cup almonds
3 cloves garlic
2 cups spinach
1 oz. basil
3/4 cup grated Parmesan cheese
2/3 cup olive oil
1 tsp. each salt and pepper

NOTES

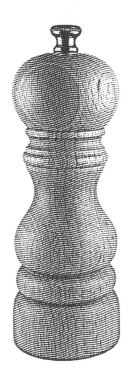

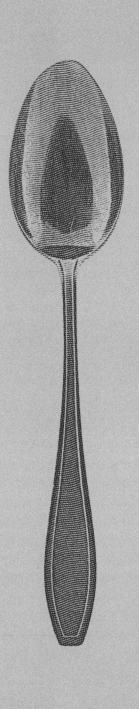

soups

In 2003, the *Des Moines Register* announced that Fort Madison would once again be the ending destination for RAGBRAI. This time we would be prepared. We had a set menu, made a lot of items ahead of time, and welcomed the riders and support staff. We dished out good food, lots of humor and, of course, the Ivy brand of hospitality.

Several months ahead of the actual ride, two men from the Chicago area drove the route looking for extra perks and finalizing details for their bicycle club in Chicago—The Chicago Urban Bicycling Society (CUBS). They stopped at the Ivy one morning, sampled our breakfast pastries, visited with our local coffee group, and then were on their way. A couple of weeks later, one of the gentlemen called and placed an order for 67 cinnamon rolls and 67 blackberry scones for the CUBS bicycle club on the last day of RAGBRAI!

The day of the race, we received a phone call to alert us that the bikers were in close proximity to the Ivy. We wheeled our baker's cart overflowing with rolls and scones to the street. The CUBS rode by single file and we handed them our pastries as they finished the last two blocks of their epic 485-mile journey across Iowa.

A year later, we discovered that one of those men, Mike Conklin, was a reporter for the *Chicago Tribune*. Mike called to say he was going to be in the area to do some bicycling and wanted to do an article for the *Tribune* about the Ivy while in the vicinity. Naturally we agreed. We served Mike and his company an evening meal, and had the opportunity to get to know them. It was an incredible evening, and Mike was very generous with ideas for marketing the Ivy. "The Ivy will soon be ten years old. You need a website and a cookbook!"

The article appeared in the Tempo Section of the *Chicago Tribune* in June 2004. The timing was perfect for the tourist scene. That summer we opened our doors to about 1,000 extra visitors who had read the article. We developed our website, www.ivybakeshoppe.com, with the help of Lee Vandenberg (in exchange for lots of caramel apple tarts), and you are obviously reading the cookbook! Thanks for the shove, Mike.

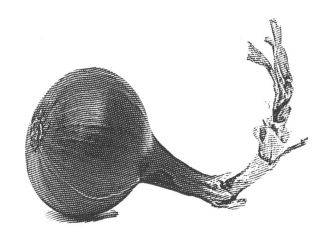

TORTILLA SOUP

Saute onion and garlic in butter in a stockpot until onion is translucent and garlic is fragrant. Add remaining ingredients and simmer at least 1 1/2 hours. Remove bay leaves and then serve with tortilla strips, sour cream, and avocado. Makes 6 to 8 servings.

Note: To make tortilla strips, cut flour tortillas in thin strips and bake at 350 degrees until crisp, about 10 to 15 minutes.

1 cup chopped onion
2 cloves garlic, chopped
4 tbsp. butter
1 cup diced red bell pepper
½ tsp. coarse black pepper
4 bay leaves
4 cups cooked,
   shredded chicken
32 oz. picante sauce
8 chicken bouillon cubes
8 cups water

BOBBY BOUNDS' FRENCH ONION SOUP

Melt butter and saute onions for 1 1/2 hours over low heat. Add next four ingredients and then saute for 10 minutes. Add broth, wine, and salt and then simmer for 2 hours; refrigerate overnight. Remove bay leaf before serving.

Reheat to serve. Place croutons or slice of French bread in bottom of a bowl or cup. Top with soup and sprinkle Swiss cheese on top. Place under broiler for 1 to 2 minutes or until cheese melts. Makes 8 to 10 servings.

1 stick butter
3 lb. peeled onions, sliced
1 ½ tsp. coarse ground
   pepper
2 tbsp. paprika
1 bay leaf
¾ cup flour
3 qt. beef broth
1 cup white wine
2 tsp. salt
French bread or croutons
½ lb. Swiss cheese, grated

GOURMET SPINACH SOUP

1 ½ sticks butter

2 small leeks, white and
light green parts only,
thinly sliced

1 cup flour

4 cups chicken broth

2 (8-oz.) pkg. cream cheese,
room temperature

3 cups cream

3 cups half-and-half

1 ½ tsp. salt

1 tsp. pepper

3 cups grated
Swiss cheese

2 lb. fresh spinach, pulsed
in food processor briefly,
or thinly sliced

Melt butter in a saucepan and then slowly saute leeks until tender. Add flour and stir until cooked. Whisk in chicken broth and stir until thickened. Add cream cheese and cream and stir until melted. Add half-and-half, salt, pepper, and Swiss cheese. Stir until melted and smooth, bringing to serving temperature slowly. Add spinach and stir until heated thoroughly. Makes 12 to 15 servings.

WHITE BEAN SOUP

3 tbsp. olive oil

2 leeks, white and light
green only, thinly sliced

3 cloves garlic, chopped

2 (15-oz.) cans white, navy,
or cannellini beans,

2 cups chicken broth

2 (15-oz.) cans chick peas,
drained and rinsed

½ tsp. ground rosemary

3 cups half-and-half

Fresh spinach for garnish

Heat olive oil in a soup pot and saute leeks and garlic over low heat until tender and fragrant. Drain and rinse beans. Add broth, beans, and rosemary and then bring to a boil. Reduce and simmer 15 minutes. Puree mixture in a food processor or blender with half-and-half. Return to stove and heat to serving temperature. Garnish with chopped fresh spinach. Makes 8 servings.

ROASTED RED PEPPER SOUP

Preheat oven to 350 degrees. Place the peppers on a large, lightly oiled baking sheet. Cook, turning every 15 minutes, for about 45 minutes, or until skins pucker and char. Remove from oven, and place in paper bags for 10 minutes. Once cooled, skins should peel very easily. Core and slice peppers.

In a soup pot, melt the butter. Add the onion, garlic, salt, pepper, and cumin. Cook slowly over low heat until onions wilt, about 10 minutes. Add bell peppers, stir, and cover, cooking for 15 minutes. Stir in flour and cook for 5 minutes. Add stock and cook another 10 minutes; remove from heat. Using a blender or food processor, puree mixture in batches with cream mixture. Return pureed soup to pot and heat slowly over low heat. Serve with a small dollop of sour cream and a sprig of cilantro on top of soup. Makes 1 gallon.

12 red bell peppers
5 tbsp. butter
5 cups chopped onion
5 cloves garlic, chopped
2 tbsp. coarse salt
1 tbsp. coarse ground pepper
1 ½ tbsp. ground cumin
⅓ cup flour
3 cups chicken stock
3 cups cream combined with 2 cups milk
Sour cream and cilantro for garnish

CREAM OF ASPARAGUS

2 leeks, white and light
  green parts, coarsely
  chopped
¼ cup olive oil
2 tsp. salt
1 tsp. pepper
1 tsp. dill weed
1 tsp. dried basil
1 tsp. dried thyme
¼ lb. carrots, peeled
  and coarsely chopped
1 qt. chicken broth
3 potatoes, peeled
  and coarsely chopped
2 (10-oz.) packages frozen
  chopped asparagus
2 cups heavy cream
2 cups half-and-half

Place leeks in a bowl and fill with water to rinse thoroughly. Lift the leeks out of the water and saute with oil, salt, pepper, and herbs in a stockpot until leeks are limp. Stir in carrots and continue to saute until they brighten. Add the chicken broth and potatoes. Bring to a boil, reduce to a simmer, and cook until potatoes are tender, but not over-cooked. Add the asparagus to the pot and continue simmering. Puree the soup with the cream in batches. Add the half-and-half and gently reheat, adjusting seasonings. Add fresh asparagus tips for garnish. Makes 8 to 12 servings.

VISCHYSSOISE

3 leeks, white and light
  green parts only,
  chopped
3 green onions, chopped
8 potatoes, peeled
  and diced
2 qt. chicken broth
2 ⅔ cups heavy cream
Salt and white pepper
Parsley

Cook the first four ingredients together for 30 minutes, or until potatoes are soft. Puree mixture in a blender or food processor with the cream until smooth. Add salt and pepper to taste; reheat. Garnish with snipped parsley. Makes 8 to 10 servings.

JUDY'S MUSHROOM BISQUE

Melt butter in a soup pot and saute mushrooms, onions, and garlic for 5 minutes, stirring constantly. Sprinkle with lemon juice. Blend in flour and stir constantly to allow the flour to cook, about 3 minutes. Stir in chicken broth and pepper slowly. Cook over low heat, stirring constantly until soup is slightly thickened. Stir in cream and heat thoroughly. Adjust seasoning to taste. Sprinkle with chopped parsley and serve. Makes 8 servings.

1 stick butter
1 ½ lb. mushrooms, thinly sliced
⅔ cup finely chopped green onions
2 cloves garlic, chopped
2 tbsp. fresh lemon juice
½ cup flour
8 cups chicken broth
1 tsp. white pepper
4 cups whipping cream
Parsley for garnish

BLACK BEAN SOUP

Soak dried beans in a gallon jug with water overnight; drain and rinse beans. Add beans and 3 quarts water to a soup pot and bring to a boil. Simmer for 3 hours, or until beans are soft, adding water if needed to keep beans covered. While stirring, mash some of beans.

Saute onion in olive oil until translucent and then add to beans. Stir in tomatoes and oil; heat thoroughly. Garnish with a dollop of sour cream. Makes 8 to 10 servings.

4 cups dried black beans
2 cups chopped onion
2 tbsp. olive oil
2 (10-oz.) cans chopped tomatoes with green chiles and lime
½ cup vegetable oil

ROASTED BUTTERNUT SQUASH SOUP

3 butternut squash,
  peeled and diced
1 cup carrots, peeled
  and diced
1 cup coarsely chopped
  red onion
2 tbsp. olive oil
4 cups chicken broth
1 ½ cups cream
2 tsp. coarse salt
¼ tsp. cayenne pepper

Toss vegetables with olive oil. Place squash and carrots on a greased baking sheet and roast at 425 degrees for 15 minutes. Add onion and continue roasting for 10 minutes more. Remove from oven and puree mixture in batches with chicken broth and cream. Add seasonings and heat on stove thoroughly. Makes 8 servings.

ACORN SQUASH SOUP

2 medium acorn squash
½ lb. leeks, white and light
  green parts only
½ stick butter
¼ tsp. dried thyme
¼ tsp. ground nutmeg
½ tsp. cinnamon
2 bay leaves
3 carrots, chopped
5 stalks celery, chopped
6 cups chicken broth
1 potato coarsely chopped
½ cup apple juice
1 ½ cups heavy cream

Slice squash in half and remove seeds. Bake cut side down in a glass casserole dish with ¹/₂ inch water. Bake at 350 degrees for 45 to 60 minutes, or until soft. Remove pulp and then set aside; discard shells.

Saute leeks in butter until soft. Add the spices and continue sauteing until leeks are transparent. Add carrots, celery, broth, and potato; bring to a boil and then simmer, covered, until the vegetables are tender. Remove the bay leaves. In a blender or food processor, puree mixture with squash, apple juice, and cream in batches until smooth. Taste for salt and pepper. Reheat gently. Makes 8 to 12 servings.

HANNAH'S LENTIL SOUP

Melt the butter in a soup pot and saute onion, garlic, carrots, and celery. Add the next seven ingredients. Bring to a boil and then add bouillon cubes and tomatoes. Simmer at least 2 hours, stirring occasionally and mashing some of the beans. If using a ham bone, take it out, cut meat off of the bone and return meat to pot. It is a thick soup and is best if made the day before serving. Remove bay leaf before serving. If too thick, the soup can be thinned with water. Freezes great. Makes 10 to 12 servings.

1 stick butter
1 large onion, chopped
2 cloves garlic, chopped
2 carrots, peeled and sliced
2 stalks celery, chopped
½ tsp. dried thyme
½ tsp. dried rosemary
1 bay leaf
½ tsp. Tabasco sauce
1 lb. dried lentil beans
2 lb. lean ham or ham bone
  with meat on it
8 cups water
8 beef bouillon cubes
1 (14-oz.) can stewed
  tomatoes

CREAM OF ZUCCHINI

Rinse leek thoroughly to remove any grit. In a tightly covered pan, simmer leek, garlic, and zucchini in butter for about 10 minutes, or until barely tender. Shake the pan occasionally to prevent sticking. Place mixture and remaining ingredients in a blender for 30 seconds. Serve either hot or cold. Makes 8 to 10 servings.

1 leek with green and white
  parts, chopped
2 cloves garlic, chopped
2 lb. small zucchini,
  thinly sliced
½ stick butter
1 tsp. salt
1 cup heavy cream
3 cups chicken broth

SPINACH POTATO SOUP

4 cups diced potatoes
3 cups chicken broth
1 tbsp. minced onion
½ tsp. garlic salt
2 cups heavy cream
¼ tsp. nutmeg
8 cups thinly sliced spinach
   (or coarsely pulsed in
   food processor)

Bring first four ingredients to a boil and then cook for 10 minutes. Add remaining ingredients except spinach and heat thoroughly. Add spinach and cook just until wilted. Makes 6 to 8 servings.

SOUTHERN SUMMER SQUASH SOUP

½ cup water
½ stick butter
2 sweet onions,
   thinly sliced
2 lb. small yellow squash,
   thinly sliced
2 lb. small zucchini,
   thinly sliced
5 medium tomatoes,
   peeled, seeded,
   and chopped
5 fresh basil leaves,
   chopped
1 tsp. salt
½ tsp. pepper

Bring water and butter to a boil in a large soup pot over medium-high heat. Add the onions, squash, and zucchini and return to a boil. Cover, reduce heat and simmer for 5 minutes. Stir in remaining ingredients. Cover and continue simmering about 5 minutes or until soup is thoroughly heated. A true taste of the first harvest! Makes 8 to 10 servings.

COLD AVOCADO SOUP

Puree the avocados with the lemon juice and broth. Place in a bowl and mix in all remaining ingredients except cream. Just before serving, add cream and stir until thoroughly combined. Garnish with a dollop of sour cream and a cilantro leaf. Makes 6 to 8 servings.

4 avocados, peeled and pitted
3 tbsp. lemon juice
1 cup chicken broth
3 green onions, thinly sliced
¼ tsp. cayenne pepper
½ tsp. coarse salt
1 tbsp. finely chopped cilantro
2 cups heavy cream

LIMA BEAN SOUP

Cook all ingredients, except half-and-half and bacon, if using, together for 25 to 30 minutes. Add half-and-half and bacon and cook until thoroughly heated. Makes 8 to 10 servings.

20 oz. frozen lima beans
1 qt. chicken broth
3 carrots, peeled and sliced
2 potatoes, peeled and diced
2 red bell peppers, cut in slivers
2 stalks celery, sliced
¼ cup butter
1 ½ tsp. marjoram
½ tsp. salt
½ tsp. pepper
½ tsp. dried oregano
2 cups half-and-half
3 strips cooked bacon, crumbled (optional)

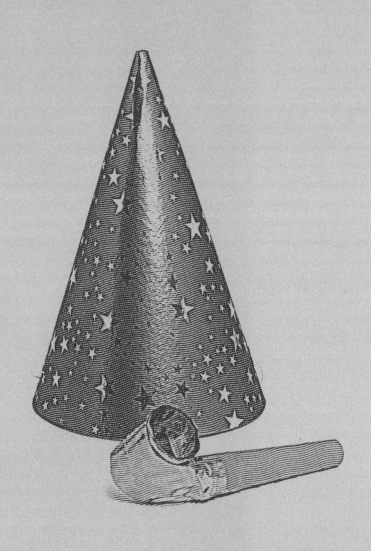

party foods

We have special recipes that we prepare for special occasions—prenuptial dinners, anniversary dinners, birthday parties, presidential campaign events, various receptions and, of course, our Valentine's Day dinner. Over the years, people have pleaded with us to open for dinner. Our workday begins at 5 a.m., so by 5 p.m. we are ready to turn into pumpkins. Sue and I have always agreed that the night scene on a regular basis would not be for us. However, when we say yes to a private party or do our annual Valentine's Day dinner, we strive to make it a special memory for all those involved—including us.

In looking back over the files of the last ten years, I am reminiscent of so many details of those parties—the Steele girls dancing to the "Macarena"; Rachel Walker's wedding cake with the vibrant red rose petals; the Pieper children's stories on the night of their parents' anniversary party; Skip's black '40 Ford parked in front of the Ivy; Steve and Elaine's engagement right before coming to our Valentine's Day dinner; the beautiful LDS brides as they come to their wedding dinner still in their gowns; the stunning decorations for the Helling/Masterson prenuptial dinner; the gathering of friends and family in remembrance of Imo Abraham, as well as the celebration of the life of John Amborn and the poem that his granddaughter wrote.

Sue and I treasure these special times. They have enriched our lives through the countless friendships and relationships made while planning these events. We have been richly rewarded. No matter how late the party, or how long the clean-up, we always manage to sit down and reflect on the goodness of the night.

MARILYN'S ORANGES

12 cups oranges,
   peeled and cut in
   bite-size pieces
2 cups water
3 cups sugar
½ cup brandy
4 tbsp. Grand Marnier or
   other orange fruit liqueur

Place oranges in a bowl and set aside. Put water and sugar in a saucepan and stir to dissolve sugar. Bring to a boil and cook 2 minutes; let cool. Add the remaining ingredients and pour over oranges; refrigerate. This should be made at least 24 to 48 hours ahead of time. Makes 12 to 15 servings.

KIWI SORBET

4 kiwi, peeled
6 oz. frozen limeade
2 cups water

Puree all of the ingredients together in a food processor. Process in a sorbet machine (or ice cream machine) for 20 minutes. Healthy and refreshing. Makes 8 servings.

BURGUNDY MUSHROOMS

Put all of the ingredients, except mushrooms, in a Dutch oven and bring to a boil. Add the mushrooms and then reduce heat to a simmer; cook 5 to 6 hours, covered. Remove lid and simmer 3 to 5 hours, or until liquid barely covers mushrooms. Serve in a chafing dish with a small amount of the liquid, or at room temperature. Freezes well and will keep for a week in the refrigerator. Makes 16 to 20 appetizers.

2 cups butter

1 qt. burgundy

1 ½ tbsp. Worcestershire sauce

1 tsp. dill weed

1 tsp. black pepper

1 tbsp. Lawry's seasoned salt

1 tsp. garlic powder

2 cups boiling water

4 beef bouillon cubes

4 chicken bouillon cubes

2 tsp. salt

4 lb. mushrooms, with stems cut off

BAKED PUMPKIN

1 (2-lb.) pumpkin, able to
stand up and with few
blemishes
2 tbsp. olive oil
2 cloves garlic, chopped
1 cup croutons, divided
1 cup grated Swiss cheese
½ cup grated
mozzarella cheese
1 ½ cups cream
1 tsp. salt
1 tsp. garlic pepper

Preheat oven to 350 degrees. Cut 2 inches off the top of the pumpkin; set aside. Remove all the pumpkin seeds. Combine the oil and garlic and then rub the mixture throughout the pumpkin and on the inside of the lid, leaving all the garlic inside the pumpkin. Place on a baking sheet.

Place one-third of croutons in bottom of pumpkin. Combine cheeses, and sprinkle $1/3$ cup over croutons. Repeat layers two more times. Mix cream, salt, and garlic pepper together and then pour into pumpkin, very slowly. Let settle if all doesn't fit, and then add rest of cream mixture. Put the top on the pumpkin and bake for 1 $1/2$ to 2 hours. Stir after 1 hour, scraping the pumpkin, if cooked, into the cheese mixture. Cook longer if pumpkin is not soft. Be careful not to puncture.

Remove from oven and stir pumpkin again. Let rest 10 minutes. With a spatula, carefully move to serving plate. Serve with crackers. Makes 20 appetizers.

Note: This recipe can be adapted and used with any size pumpkin.

BECKY'S SPINACH ARTICHOKE PHYLLO

Mix the first seven ingredients together to combine. Generously butter one sheet of phyllo, top with another sheet of phyllo and butter it also. Keep a damp cloth on top of remaining phyllo so it doesn't dry out. Cut the buttered phyllo into 8 strips. Place I teaspoon spinach mixture on each piece at the bottom and then fold as if folding a flag. Freeze until ready to use. To serve right from freezer, bake at 375 degrees for 15 minutes, or until golden brown. Makes about 4 dozen.

3 oz. fresh spinach, pulsed in food processor 5 pulses

1 cup artichoke hearts, drained and chopped

½ cup mayonnaise

½ cup grated Parmesan cheese

1 tsp. onion salt

1 tsp. garlic powder

½ tsp. pepper

Melted butter

1 pkg. phyllo, thawed in refrigerator

ADRIAN'S DELIGHT

Cream the first three ingredients together until combined and then add sugar. Soften gelatin in cold water by stirring over hot water. Add gelatin mixture to the cream cheese mixture. Add the remaining ingredients. Pour into a 4-cup mold or plastic container lined with plastic wrap. Refrigerate and turn out onto a serving platter; remove plastic wrap. Serve with saltine crackers. Freezes well. Makes 24 appetizers.

1 ½)8-oz.) pkg cream cheese, room temperature

1 stick butter, room temperature

½ cup sour cream

½ cup sugar

1 pkg. unflavored gelatin

¼ cup cold water

½ cup Craisins

1 cup toasted sliced almonds

Zest of 2 lemons

COLD ROTEL DIP

2 (8-oz.) pkg. cream
cheese, room
temperature
1 can diced tomatoes with
green peppers, juice
reserved

Blend cream cheese with the tomato juice and process in a food processor or blender until smooth. Stir in the tomatoes with peppers. Serve with a tostado or tortilla chips. Makes 10 to 12 servings.

TOMATO BASIL DIP

1 cup mayonnaise
½ cup sour cream
½ cup fresh chopped basil
1 tbsp. tomato paste
1 tbsp. lemon zest

Whisk all ingredients together until well blended. Chill up to 2 days. Use for dip with blanched or roasted fresh green beans or fresh asparagus. Makes 1 $^1/_2$ pounds.

PATTY'S PARTY MIX

Place the first five ingredients in a large roasting pan. Melt the butter in a saucepan and stir in remaining ingredients. Pour over cereal mixture and stir thoroughly to coat. Bake at 250 degrees for 2 hours, stirring every 15 minutes. Makes 30 servings.

2 (15-oz.) pkg. corn, rice, or wheat cereal
1 (10- to 12-oz.) pkg. pretzels
1 (15-oz.) pkg. toasted oats cereal
1 lb. mixed nuts
1 lb. cocktail peanuts
4 sticks butter
2 tbsp. Worcestershire sauce
2 tsp. garlic salt
3 tsp. celery salt
2 tsp. onion salt

GRANNY HIGBY'S LEMON SHERBET

Mix all the ingredients together. I know this is lemon sherbet, but Granny Higby always added 2 drops of green food coloring.

In Granny Higby's recipe, put mixture into freezer trays, and freeze until slushy, beat, and freeze again; repeat.

The Ivy way is once it is all mixed together, put into ice cream machine and process for 20 minutes. Ready to serve or put in cups and freeze. It is delicious! A delightful refreshing afternoon treat with lace or sugar cookies for company, or serve anytime for family. Makes 16 servings.

4 cups milk
Juice of 3 lemons (about 8 tbsp.)
2 cups sugar

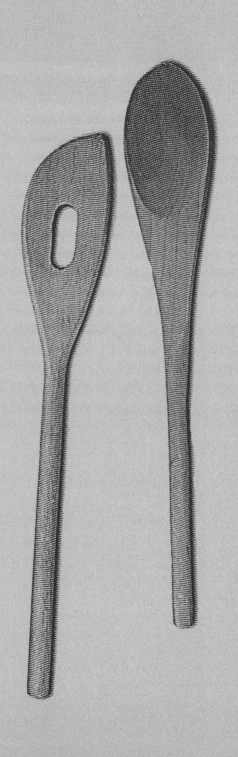

—— salads ——

I f you are standing still, you are falling behind. That adage certainly applies to the restaurant industry. You cannot rest on your laurels, or customers' favorites. We started this cafe based on a fresh, eclectic, and creative menu. In order to keep that reputation, we are constantly forced to think outside of the box.

Over the last couple of years, we have added cooking classes, a bistro menu, paninis, and great fresh salad combinations with house-made dressings. With American's desire to eat healthier, we have created some entrees and side dishes with fewer calories, lower carbohydrates, less fat, and/or more grains. In doing so, we haven't sacrificed the taste, and have actually impacted people who aren't trying to eat healthier. They choose these light selections simply because they taste so good. The state of Iowa recently started an initiative called "The Shape of Iowa," encouraging Iowans to watch their weight. We responded by adding a Lighten Up Iowa offering, which has also proven to be wildly successful.

So, there you have it! For Sue and me, the Ivy has been successful because we are doing what we love. We are empowered every single day by a customer enjoying our food, our atmosphere, or just building a memory. For him or her to say "thank you" is just icing on the cake. We can't help but feel immense pride when the CEO from Bagcraft, Scott's, Dial, or Dupont visits Fort Madison and the Ivy, and takes home a Caramel Apple Tart for their family's dinner that night in Chicago, Arizona, or Delaware; or to entertain the world marketing team of a local industry, knowing they are returning to their homes in England, Brazil, Ukraine, or New Zealand to tell their family and neighbors about the meal they had at the Ivy.

Our staff is so much a part of the Ivy's success. We have empowered our staff to know that they make a difference. We constantly tell them that it takes all of us to give the customers what they want: the friendliness of the staff, the warm, glorious atmosphere of the restaurant, the gorgeous presentation of the meal, and the sumptuous fresh taste of the food. The customers expect the finest, and we deliver. Working together with our staff, Sue and I have created a marvelous restaurant, where memories are being made, friendships forged, and great food served.

And in the end, things have a way of working out for the best.

CHICKEN SALAD

Mix the first seven ingredients together and combine thoroughly. Add lemon juice and seasonings. Makes great sandwiches or good on a bed of lettuce, or stuffed in a tomato. Makes about 2 quarts.

1 ½ lb. cooked chicken, chopped
4 stalks celery, diced
⅓ cup sliced black olives
¼ cup crushed pineapple, drained
¼ cup pimientos
1 cup mayonnaise (not Miracle Whip)
3 tbsp. Durkee's mustard sauce
Juice of 1 lemon
2 tsp. dill weed
1 ½ tsp. salt and pepper

CHICKEN-GRAPE SALAD

Mix the first three ingredients together in a bowl. In a smaller bowl, stir mayonnaise, lemon juice, and seasonings together. Mix with chicken mixture and adjust seasonings as needed. Garnish with toasted pecans. Makes 8 servings.

5 cups cooked, chopped chicken
2 cups green or red grapes, cut in half
1 cup diced celery
1 ½ cups mayonnaise
2 tbsp. lemon juice
1 tsp. coarse pepper
2 tsp. celery salt
Toasted pecans

CHICKEN WALDORF SALAD

DRESSING

¾ cup white balsamic
   vinegar
¾ cup orange juice
2 tsp. coarse salt
1 tsp. pepper
2 tbsp. Dijon mustard
1 ¼ cups olive oil

SALAD

5 whole chicken breasts,
   baked and chopped
2 cups Craisins
5 stalks celery, diced
2 ½ cups chopped pecans,
   toasted
3 apples, cored and
   coarsely chopped with
   peeling on
Leaf lettuce or mixed
   greens

For the dressing, blend the first five ingredients together in a food processor. With the machine running, slowly add olive oil in a thin stream; set aside.

For the salad, place the chicken, Craisins, and celery in a bowl. Add three-fourths of the dressing and toss to coat. Cover and refrigerate 3 to 4 hours. Just before serving, add the pecans and apples. Add remaining dressing if needed and then serve over lettuce. Makes 12 to 15 servings.

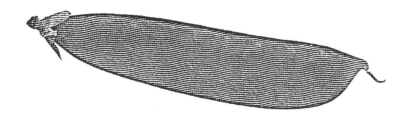

HOT CHICKEN SALAD

Preheat oven to 400 degrees. Combine chicken, celery, onion, mayonnaise, and pecans in a bowl and stir well. Spread mixture in a greased 9 x 13-inch glass dish. Combine potato chips and cheddar cheese and sprinkle over chicken mixture. Bake for 30 minutes, or until heated through. Makes 8 servings.

6 cups cooked, chopped chicken
3 cups thinly sliced celery
½ cup diced onion
2 cups mayonnaise
1 cup pecans, toasted
1 ½ cups crushed potato chips
3 cups grated cheddar cheese

SUMMER PASTA MEDLEY

Cook the noodles according to package directions; let cool. Lightly toss together all of the vegetables. For the dressing, mix the Dijon mustard and remaining ingredients together until fully incorporated. Pour over vegetables and then add the pasta. Mix gently but thoroughly. Serve with sprigs of fresh parsley. Makes 8 to 10 servings.

1 lb. linguini noodles
1 cup snow peas, blanched for 1 minute
1 cup artichoke hearts, cut in half
1 cup green olives
1 red bell pepper, juilienned
1 small zucchini, juilienned
1 cup chopped parsley

DRESSING
2 tsp. Dijon mustard
½ tsp. curry powder
3 tbsp. red wine vinegar
½ cup olive oil
1 tsp. garlic salt
1 tsp. pepper

GREEN BEAN-ARTICHOKE SALAD

½ lb. fresh green beans
½ cup cut-up cauliflower
3 green onions, chopped
½ red bell pepper, sliced
in strips and cut in half
2 carrots, peeled and
coined on diagonal
1 (8-oz.) can water
chestnuts, drained
1 cup artichoke hearts,
cut in half

DRESSING
¼ cup Italian dressing
2 tbsp. red wine vinegar
2 tbsp. garlic pepper

Blanch the green beans in boiling water for 4 minutes. Immediately rinse in cold water to stop the cooking. Cut beans in thirds. Stir rest of ingredients together, adding the green beans once they are cool. Mix the dressing ingredients together and then toss with salad. We have also added rotini garden pasta to make a great main dish pasta salad. Makes 8 servings.

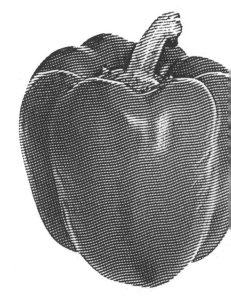

GUACAMOLE SALAD

Tear all the lettuce into bite-size pieces and combine with onions; set in the refrigerator. To make dressing, combine all the ingredients in a food processor or blender and puree until smooth.

To serve, place lettuce mixture in large bowl and top with tomatoes, black beans, and cheeses. Serve with dressing and tortilla chips. Makes 4 to 6 servings.

1 head romaine lettuce
½ head iceberg lettuce
½ cup chopped
   green onions
½ cup diced tomatoes
1 cup black beans,
   rinsed and drained
¼ cup grated
   cheddar cheese
¼ cup grated
   Monterey Jack cheese

Tri-color tortilla chips

DRESSING
1 avocado, peeled, pitted,
   and mashed
1 tbsp. fresh lemon juice
½ cup sour cream
⅓ cup vegetable oil
1 tbsp. picante sauce

SPINACH SALAD

DRESSING
3 tbsp. lemon juice
2 tsp. Dijon mustard
2 ½ tbsp. honey
½ cup olive oil

SALAD
½ cup thinly sliced
  red onion rings
1 cup red wine vinegar
3 tbsp. sugar
6 oz. fresh spinach
¼ cup crumbled
  cooked bacon
¼ cup toasted pecans
½ cup grated Asiago
  cheese
Fresh strawberry slices
  (when in season)
  or mandarin oranges

For the dressing, place the first three ingredients in a blender and mix together. With the machine running, slowly add the olive oil in a thin stream until combined.

Thinly slice onion using a mandolin. Combine red wine vinegar and sugar. Stir in onions and marinate at least 2 hours. Place spinach on a plate. Spread onions over greens, and then top with bacon, pecans, and Asiago cheese. Place sliced strawberries or mandarin oranges on top. Drizzle dressing over salad. Makes 2 servings.

SPRING FLING

Open ramen noodles and save seasoning packet for another use. Break up the noodles and mix with the almonds on a baking sheet; drizzle with butter. Bake at 350 degrees for 10 minutes, or until golden, stirring after 5 minutes; let cool.

For the dressing, mix all the ingredients together in a jar and shake until well combined.

To assemble, place the mixed greens on a plate. Sprinkle with feta cheese and ramen noodle mixture. Place strawberries over top. Drizzle dressing over salad. Makes 4 to 5 servings.

1 pkg. ramen noodles
½ cup sliced almonds
2 tbsp. butter, melted
12 oz. mixed greens
1 ½ cup crumbled
　feta cheese
Sliced strawberries

DRESSING
½ cup oil
¼ cup red wine vinegar
½ tsp. salt
½ tsp. sugar
¼ tsp. pepper
2 tsp. cream
1 tbsp. poppy seeds

TOMATO-CUCUMBER SALAD WITH FETA

Peel cucumbers, leaving some strips of the peel. Cut in half lengthwise, seed, and then cut in chunks. Cut cherry tomatoes in half. Gently stir all the ingredients together in a bowl and chill 1 hour or more before serving. Makes 6 to 8 servings.

3 small cucumbers
8 cherry tomatoes
2 cups crumbled
　feta cheese
4 green onions,
　thinly sliced
¼ cup white
　balsamic vinegar
1 tbsp. chopped fresh basil
1 ½ tsp. garlic salt

CRANBERRY SALAD

1 pkg. unflavored gelatin
¼ cup cold water
2 cups boiling water
2 pkg. sugar-free gelatin
   (raspberry, strawberry,
   or cranberry)
1 (12-oz.) pkg. cranberries,
   coarsely chopped in a
   food processor
2 apples, chopped
   with peel
2 oranges, peeled
   and chopped
1 cup crushed pineapple,
   drained
½ cup chopped celery
Juice of 1 lemon

Mix unflavored gelatin with cold water to dissolve; set aside. Add 2 cups boiling water to flavored gelatin. Stir until gelatin is dissolved and then add the softened unflavored gelatin.

Place cranberries, apples, oranges, pineapple, celery, and lemon juice in a big bowl and pour gelatin mixture over top; stir until combined. Pour into a 9 x 13-inch glass dish, making sure the gelatin covers all the fruit. Chill until firm. Makes 8 to 12 servings.

index

Metric Conversion Chart

Liquid and Dry Measures

U.S.	Canadian	Australian
1/4 teaspoon	1 mL	1 ml
1/2 teaspoon	2 mL	2 ml
1 teaspoon	5 mL	5 ml
1 Tablespoon	15 mL	20 ml
1/4 cup	50 mL	60 ml
1/3 cup	75 mL	80 ml
1/2 cup	125 mL	125 ml
2/3 cup	150 mL	170 ml
3/4 cup	175 mL	190 ml
1 cup	250 mL	250 ml
1 quart	1 liter	1 litre

Temperature Conversion Chart

Fahrenheit	Celsius
250	120
275	140
300	150
325	160
350	180
375	190
400	200
425	220
450	230
475	240
500	260